A PACKET OF SURPRISES:

THE BEST ESSAYS AND SERMONS OF F. W. BOREHAM

BY

F. W. BOREHAM

JOHN BROADBANKS PUBLISHING
EUREKA, CA 2008

John Broadbanks Publishing
Eureka, CA
2008

10 9 8 7 6 5 4 3 2 1

Printed in the United States of America

ISBN-13 978-0-9790334-4-5
ISBN-10 0-9790334-4-6

Proof Reader: Bryan Gish
Cover Designer: Laura Zugzda
Typographer: Stephanie Martindale

Second Edition, 2012

PUBLISHED BY
JOHN BROADBANKS PUBLISHING

F. W. Boreham

A Packet of Surprises: The Best Essays and Sermons of F. W. Boreham

All the Blessings of Life: The Best Stories of F. W. Boreham (Revised)

Angels, Palms and Fragrant Flowers: F. W. Boreham on C. H. Spurgeon

From England to Mosgiel

In Pastures Green: A Ramble through the Twenty-third Psalm

Loose Leaves: A Travel Journal

Lover of Life: F. W. Boreham's Tribute to His Mentor (Revised and Expanded)

Second Thoughts —Introduction by Ravi Zacharias

The Chalice of Life: Reflections on the Significant Stages in Life

Geoff Pound

Making Life Decisions: Journey in Discernment

Talk About Thanksgiving: Stories of Gratitude

Jeff Cranston

Happily Ever After: Studies in the Beatitudes

A PACKET OF SURPRISES

On the other planets things happen according to rote;
you can see with half an eye what is coming next. But this
world is a box of tricks, a packet of surprises. You never
know one minute what the next minute holds in store.
Everything is effervescent, full of snap and sparkle.

F. W. Boreham, *The Silver Shadow*, 12.

CONTENTS

PREFACE

SELECTING THE BEST

Choosing the best essays of F. W. Boreham is as excruciating as selecting some children to get the honors and telling the others that they did not make the grade. As mentioned in the preface to *All the Blessings of Life: The Best Stories of F. W. Boreham* the selection is subjective. But there is some rhyme and reason to the choices. Some were voted in by current Boreham readers so they appear by popular demand. Others are clearly Boreham's choice or were popular in his day. His biographer, T. Howard Crago, reported that "The Other Side of the Hill" (a variation of which was entitled "The Sunny Side of the Ranges," was an address delivered 80 times, and "The House that Jack Built" was given 140 times to churches that requested Dr. Boreham to give this lecture to their community as a fund raiser.[1]

---

[1] T. Howard Crago, *The Story of F. W. Boreham* (London: Marshall, Morgan & Scott, 1961), 172-174.

In compiling this selection an effort has been made to include essays on a range of themes, those which illustrate different homiletical methods and others that are drawn from different periods in Boreham's career. The sermons, "Mind Your Own Business," "He Made as Though" and "A Prophet's Pilgrimage" represent extensive reflections on Biblical stories. The chapters entitled, "Dominoes," "Please Shut the Gate!" and "I.O.U." are fine examples of the way F. W. Boreham told parables by taking ordinary, everyday objects or expressions and skillfully helping his hearers to discover a deeper truth. The messages on the favorite texts of Catherine Booth, Fyodor Dostoyevsky and Abraham Lincoln are representative of the 100+ addresses in the most popular Boreham sermon series that are contained in the five books on the theme, "Texts that Made History." "The Squirrel's Dream" and "Waiting for the Tide" offer glimpses into the way F. W. Boreham used paintings to illustrate his themes.

The sermon "The Whisper of God" may at face value have not made the cut in Boreham's best but it is included because it is the best of his earliest sermons and it illustrates how his preaching changed in style, structure and length. His contemporary, J. J. North, judged Boreham's early literary ventures to be "long-worded" because "the terse Boreham had not arrived."[2] Amid the many admiring reviews, it was said of Boreham's first volume of sermons, *The Whisper of God,* that "if illustrations and incidents did not jostle so thickly on the pages and the poetical quotations were remorselessly reduced the sermons would gain

---

[2] J. J. North, *New Zealand Baptist,* April 1943.

much in value."[3] *The Best Essays of F. W. Boreham* demonstrates the way that Boreham worked hard to remodel his writing and preaching through such things as the removal of wordy clutter, for it is clear to see the emergence of a simple and flowing style.

GENRE

Already the terms "essay," "sermon," "lecture" and "address" have been used in this introduction. Some of the chapters in his books are clearly one genre or another but F. W. Boreham was, as Lindsay Newnham described, the great "recycler" who suited his style to his audience and tweaked his material to fit the allotted time or word limits.[4]

In a review of the book *A Bunch of Everlastings*, Dr. James Hastings, editor of the famous *Dictionary of the Bible*, asked a question that many readers have asked: "Is Mr. Boreham able to preach such sermons as these, exactly as they are printed here? Their interest is undoubted and intense. For Mr. Boreham is an artist. Every sermon is constructed. Every thought is in its place, and appropriately expressed. And there are no marks left in the constructing. To the literary student, as to the average reader of sermons, every sermon is literature." Howard Crago, (whose text was read by F. W. Boreham) answered, "The fact was, of course, that each of these sermons was preached from memory in almost the exact words in which it was printed."[5]

---

[3] Review of *Whisper of God*, (n.p., n.d.). This review appears in a clipping that Boreham kept in his own copy of *Whisper of God*.

[4] Lindsay L. Newnham, "Recycling by Dr. F. W. Boreham," *Our Yesterdays* 5 (Melbourne: Victorian Baptist Historical Society, 1997), 78.

[5] T. Howard Crago, *The Story of F. W. Boreham*, 179.

TRUTH THROUGH PERSONALITY

If the content of these sermons and lectures were word for word the same as what we read in this volume they do not convey fully the total impact of the preaching event—the pausing, the modulation of his voice, the twinkle in the eye and the response of his hearers. Fortunately Howard Crago has recorded this colorful insight into how one of F. W. Boreham's addresses was received:

> As time went on and "The House That Jack Built" grew in popularity, the lecturer developed it and perfected its delivery until the whole thing flowed on for more than an hour of fascinating elocution and magnificent eloquence. He himself revelled in reciting it, and the audience enjoyed it to the full while being unconsciously influenced by its gentle suggestiveness.

> A typical audience-reaction was that of the Rev. C. Bernard Cockett, M.A., who, after hearing the lecture in a Surrey Hills church said, "It is not to be wondered at that individuals who appreciate the words of an author are interested in him as a man, lecturer and minister. Therefore, when the Rev. F. W. Boreham's presence was heralded in a Melbourne suburb many people asked, "What is he like? Can he speak and preach as well as write? Has he personality and originality in the pulpit as well as in the study?" Boreham came, spoke, and conquered! He spoke for an hour; but the minutes passed by on shimmering wings. He speaks quite as well as he writes—the voice is strong and

sweet; ringing, yet winning, and the word lives in
the message. "The House That Jack Built" was
a brilliant drama, staged and performed by the
author. And his control of the audience! A happy
and original introduction; apposite stories from
history, science, and romance, related with telling effect; soft touches on the varying notes of
the human soul, making it tremble with childlike
laughter, and then a sudden chord of richer music
with concentrated and arresting power—while
the listener perceives God through smiles.

Moving a vote of thanks at Wangaratta [Victo-
ria], a local farmer expressed a good deal when
he said, "I enjoyed the lecture because I could
see that Mr. Boreham was enjoying it so much
himself."[6]

INFLAMING PASSION
These essays and sermons have been brought together not
for literary inspection and homiletical interest but so they
might speak powerfully to readers in this contemporary
age. F. W. Boreham believed in the importance of heroes,
he devoted an entire chapter of his autobiography to two
of his preaching models[7] and he encouraged preachers to
study evangelistic models to "inflame your devotion."[8]

---

[6] T. Howard Crago, *The Story of F. W. Boreham,* 172-173.

[7] F. W. Boreham, *My Pilgrimage* (London: The Epworth Press, 1940),
98-103.

[8] F. W. Boreham, *I Forgot to Say,* 42.

But Boreham sounded a warning about copying the style of someone else. Writing on the topic, "A troop of apes," he drew analogies from nature (lyre bird, jays, ostriches and apes) to state that, "life abounds in mimicry" and if our tendency to imitation is so strong and impossible to eradicate, then human beings must select "worthy models."[9]

BE YOURSELF

The great hope for this new book is that it might stimulate among its readers one of the major themes of F. W. Boreham—that each person, with their God-given gifts might develop their unique style:

> He sees as nobody else sees. He must therefore paint or preach or pray or write as nobody else does. He must be himself: must see with his own eyes and utter that vision in the terms of his own personality.[10]

Geoff Pound

[9] F. W. Boreham, *Mercury,* October 8, 1955.
[10] F. W. Boreham, *Mercury,* September 9, 1950.

THE REV. DR. F. W. BOREHAM OBE: A PROFILE

BY THE REV T. HOWARD CRAGO

This address was presented to the Victorian Baptist Histori-cal Society by F. W. Boreham's biographer, the Rev T. Howard Crago, and was published by the Baptist Union of Victoria, Victorian Baptist Historical Society in 1986. Gratitude is expressed to the current Executive of this Society for permission to republish this speech in this publication.

At the General Assembly of the Church of Scotland in Edinburgh in 1928, the Moderator introduced the speaker, the Rev. F. W. Boreham, as "the man whose name is on all our lips, whose books are on all our shelves and whose illustrations are in all our sermons."

For the sake of any who did not know him, we might ask, 'Who was this person of such note?' A short reply would be that he was one of us, whose name was for some 40 years on the Ministerial List of the Baptist Union of Victoria. A complete reply would require volumes.

Frank William Boreham was born at Tunbridge Wells, Kent, on March 3, 1871, the son of devout Anglican parents. He left primary school at 14, attended night classes for a few months afterwards then went to work as a clerk in London at 17. Soon after arriving in the metropolis, he was converted to Christ—an experience that changed his life's direction and led to a sense of call to the ministry.

He occupied but three pastorates. After graduating from Spurgeon's College in London in 1895 he accepted a call to a small country Baptist church in Mosgiel, New Zealand—in a farming district inhabited largely by Scottish immigrants and their families. He was approaching 24 years of age. A reporter described him about that time as "tall, slim, with a drooping moustache and deep, dreamy eyes," but did not draw attention to the young preacher's walking with a limp, aided by the walking stick that was his invariable companion. The limp was a legacy of a railway accident in which Frank Boreham had lost a foot when he was 15.

Although of such limited education, not being physically impressive and handicapped by an artificial limb, Frank Boreham was endowed with compensating gifts, which he cultivated to the full. He possessed an observant eye, a penetrating mind, vivid visual memory, keen imagination, and an earnest evangelistic zeal.

A voracious reader, on settling in Mosgiel, he resolved to buy and read at least a book a week. He made marginal notes to help his memory, and compiled his own index in the back of each book.

He early realized that his voice was unusually high-pitched and monotonous, and that his delivery in preaching was too fast: people could not get on to his train of thought. He would therefore shut the study door and exercise his voice up and down the scale. When holidaying at the beach he would stand alone and preach to the waves. He visited law courts in nearby Dunedin at which the best barristers were addressing the jury, to study their arts of persuasion.

Thus he cultivated his slender gifts and a preaching style that was unique, and in which every distinctly uttered word carried the maximum content of meaning, clear mental imagery and feeling.

He learned to preach from but a few sermon notes. On one occasion when he had been using a large sheet of notes, wind blowing through an open window carried the notes away. Ever afterwards he would reduce the sermon outlines to a dozen words, write them boldly on a 10 cm by 15 cm paper slip, and attach it to a similar-sized piece of polished plywood. No wind was strong enough to blow that from the pulpit.

During those eleven years in Mosgiel he was storing his memory with incidents of pastoral life, many amusing, others deeply tragic, but all highly entertaining—stories he would later share with millions of readers of whom he did not at that time dream.

The congregation in the little weatherboard church at Mosgiel had never heard such interesting preaching and soon filled it to overflowing, necessitating doubling its size. Not only was the preaching entertaining, it was also helping them, and leading many to commitment to Christ.

During Mosgiel's formative years he also came to hold certain principles he was to carry right through his ministry. He would never condemn anything but always present a positive aspect. As he put it, "the best way to prove a stick is crooked is to lay a straight one beside it."

He also became convinced that if a sermon was to grip and retain the hearers' attention it must possess an "entertainment value." That did not mean, he said, that it should be humorous, nor entertain only for its own sake, for tragedy could be as entertaining as comedy. He realized that people are interested in people more than in abstract ideas. Therefore he used endless stories from experience, biography, history, literature—anywhere—believing that the best way to communicate an idea is to wrap it up in a person. For example he told me he could never preach nor write on, say, "Friendship," in the abstract. But he thought he could retell Dickens' story of David Copperfield and Agnes so that it portrayed some aspects of friendship in concrete, personal terms.

When Frank Boreham was a baby back in Tunbridge Wells, an old gipsy crone noticed him in the arms of his nanny—as she nursed him in a park. She picked up the little hand, scrutinized it, and said to the nurse, "Tell his mother to put a pen in his hand and he'll never want for a living."

Only a psychologist could decide whether or not that prognostication, which his mother often repeated to him, influenced his future. But soon after arriving in New Zealand he began supplying manuscripts of his sermons to the Mosgiel newspaper. As time went by, before submitting them, he would rewrite them in condensed form, more like essays, and in a more entertaining and readable format. He was developing the unique style that was to characterize a stream of books that were to bear his name during the ensuing years.

Soon after his arrival in Mosgiel in 1895 his sweetheart of college days, Miss Stella Cottee, had accepted his proposal of marriage and sailed to join him in New Zealand. They had five children, three of whom survive [in 1986]—Mrs. Ivy McDonald in Bendigo, Mrs. Joan Lincoln in Hobart, and son Frank, an officer of the Baptist Church at Kew.

After eleven years or so sharpening his skills with words and cultivating his preaching gifts, Frank Boreham accepted a call to the Hobart Baptist Tabernacle.

He confounded the welcoming Hobart deacons as they streamed up the ship's gangway at the Hobart dock, by greeting each one by name. He was not clairvoyant but had simply memorized their faces and names from a group photo which the secretary had sent to him.

After Mosgiel's humble sanctuary, Hobart's spacious tabernacle seemed to stretch away into infinity. His striving after excellence, practiced on the farmers and small townsfolk, blossomed under the challenge and inspiration of the larger Hobart congregation.

Close to his fortieth birthday, Frank Boreham considered that his public might welcome a volume of his essays, so from a pile of cuttings, submitted a selection of 32 to Hodder and Stoughton in London. After several weeks, a rejection slip arrived, accompanying the returned essays saying that Hodder and Stoughton did not consider the articles suitable for their publication. However, during the following years they would come almost cap in hand, begging him to supply them with the manuscript of a book.

Nothing daunted, he looked over his library for the name of another publisher who handled essays, and sent his parcel of papers to London again: to C. H. Kelly, not knowing then that Kelly, afterwards known as The Epworth Press, was the publishing house of the Methodist Church. Kelly said, yes, they would publish the book on a royalty basis, if he would personally buy 300 copies himself at half price. But what would an author do with 300 of his own book? He was about to drop his letter declining the proposal into the mail box when he bumped into a well-known Hobart bookseller to whom he confided the contents of the letter. The bookseller saved the situation and ensured Boreham's literary future. He would jump at the chance to obtain 300 copies at half price, he said. So the first Boreham book of essays, "The Luggage of Life," was launched, to be followed by some fifty other titles. Within the next few years his name was a household one throughout the Christian world.

While involved in pastoral activities, he made time to write several essays a week. On receiving proofs of an essay from the periodical in which it was to appear, he would cut the proof into sections and paste each one on a book-page-sized sheet of paper. From this mounting accumulation of paste-ups would be selected a sufficient number for the next book. There was a time when 20 such embryo books were awaiting their turn for publication.

One reviewer wrote in the "Age," "Through these volumes stride many of those old Scottish friends of Mosgiel days. Tamis, Wullie and Gavin, officers of that little church, and many others, have delighted thousands who have listened to their quaint talk and followed their romantic ways. In almost every volume are intimate tales of John Broadbanks, minister at Silverstream, whose wise words

and kind actions had a peculiar charm. Not only those
remarkable people form the subjects of Boreham's studies.
He also found lessons in the most commonplace things of
life. Ordinary creatures like asses and magpies, or mad dogs
and mosquitoes attract his fancy and under the touch of
his pen take their place among the great teachers. It is surprising what he sees in "smoke" and gets out of "pockets,"
whether he is writing on "Cranks" or "Kisses" he pours his
vast variety of ideas into a mold of colorful words."

Other demands also occupied his pen. It all began
back in his Mosgiel days when the young pastor had been
carried away by the four volumes of Gibbon's *The Decline
and Fall of the Roman Empire* and references to Gibbon
were cropping up in almost every address he delivered.
Then a casual incident was to have life-long consequences.
One night in an address to a Christian Endeavour Society in Dunedin, he contrasted the reluctance of young
men in the days of Rome's decline and fall to rally to the
empire's defense, and the eagerness with which New Zealand young men were volunteering for the South African
War which had recently started.

Following the meeting, he walked to the railway station to catch the 9:30 a.m. train back to Mosgiel only to
find he had missed it and had to fill in two hours till the
next. Wondering what to do with himself, he glanced up
and saw the windows of the offices of the "Otago Daily
Times" ablaze with light. He would go across and interview
the editor! He asked that gentleman whether he could use
any free-lance contributions in his newspaper.

The editor replied that he used only material written
by staff specialists. As the disappointed Frank Boreham

rose to leave, the editor casually mentioned that the editorial for the next morning's issue had yet to be written, and asked, "What would you say if you were to write it?" Without hesitation his visitor replied, "I would establish a contrast between the patriotic eagerness of New Zealand young men to sail for South Africa and the shameful reluctance of Rome's young men to answer the empire's call in its declining years."

Pointing to a table and chair, the editor invited his visitor to write it. Within the next 90 minutes, with the Endeavor address still echoing in his mind, Frank Boreham dashed off 1100 words, sprinkled with quotes from Gibbon, Tennyson and R. L. Stevenson. F.W.B. had missed the train to Mosgiel, but had caught the literary train. That night's composition, which he was excited to read in the next morning's editorial column, led to numerous similar contributions to the "Otago Times" and thousands of editorials, biographical profiles and other articles for leading newspapers, such as the Hobart "Mercury" every week for 46 years—and later, the Melbourne "Age" for 14 years until his death.

Soon after arriving in Hobart, Boreham had begun regular contributions to the "Southern Baptist" published in Melbourne, the forerunner of the "Australian Baptist." When the "Australian Baptist" replaced the "Southern Baptist" in 1912, its first editor arranged with him to provide a fortnightly essay for its pages. This series also continued until some time after his death 50 years later, for he had already sent a parcel of contributions—as his custom—well in advance of their publication date.

At the same time, "The Australian Christian World," published in Sydney, was reprinting by arrangement what

he wrote for the "Australian Baptist." Later, after removing
to Armadale, he accepted an invitation to write the Saturday leading article for the "Age," now entitled "A Saturday
Reflection," which he did until his death. His sermons were
still the seeds from which all these essays grew.

Under his ministry the Hobart church membership
flourished. Although his preaching was evangelistic he felt
unable to follow the then popular evangelistic method of
appealing for public confessions of faith. In each of his pastorates evangelization was on a more personal basis, arising
from what today we would call pastoral counseling, and the
regular classes he conducted for candidates for discipleship
and church membership.

Whether he was preaching in Wesley's Chapel, or the
City Temple, or the Metropolitan Tabernacle in London,
or Fifth Avenue Presbyterian Church in New York, crowds
flocked to hear him. Of few other Baptist ministers may that
be said. Nor did they come simply because he was one of
the most interesting preachers they ever heard, but because
those messages gently awakened in so many of them a deep
sense of being loved by God—a love revealed in the Cross
of Christ.

Boreham was not what you might call "a straight from
the shoulder preacher." His kind of preaching was what
the commercial world would call the "soft sell." By simply
showing how all truth led to Christ, he showed people the
way without trying to push them into it, and that many
people chose that way is seen in the fact that during his
three pastorates he was the means of doubling the membership of those churches. Later, in his 30 years of itinerating
preaching among all denominations hundreds of people
found the Savior.

This may sound as though Boreham's ministerial life consisted only of writing essays and preparing and preaching sermons. But he was also immersed in the wider work of the denomination. He was elected President of the Baptist Union of New Zealand. He was twice President of the Tasmanian Union during his eleven years in Hobart and visited the churches throughout the State. He also gave a lead in social issues, especially the temperance cause. Overseas missions were dear to his heart wherever he served. In Victoria he was elected Chairman of the Victorian Committee of the Australian Baptist Missionary Society. He was keenly interested in ministerial training and served on Candidates Boards and Theological College Councils.

At the peak of the Hobart pastorate came a call to Armadale in Victoria. It was 1917, the nation was at war and he was 46. After this memorable 11 years pastorate, remembered by many still among us, the grateful church elected him Pastor-Emeritus.

In 1928 Frank Boreham retired from Armadale to devote his remaining years to a wider ministry among all the churches and in other countries. The family moved to a home they had bought in Kew, and joined the membership of the Kew Baptist Church. F.W.B. was then 57.

Later that year, with the world as his new parish, Boreham and his lady sailed for Britain for the first leg of a four months preaching tour arranged for him by his publishers. His books were selling well around the world and his name was well-known, as Dr. Lamont so picturesquely put it to the Assembly of the Church of Scotland.

It was during this year 1928 that the McMaster University of Canada conferred upon Mr. Boreham its honorary degree of Doctor of Divinity, "in recognition of his contribution to Christian thought." An extensive preaching tour of Canada and the United States followed the British itinerary.

On returning home, the Doctor said that he had to pinch himself to make sure he was not dreaming as he had preached in the Metropolitan Tabernacle, Wesley's Chapel, the City temple and other famous pulpits.

We might have expected that what the world calls success would have gone to the Doctor's head, but those who remember him know that he remained a modest and humble person to the end.

Perhaps Dr. Boreham's most important ministry in many ways was the Wednesday lunch-hour services he conducted in Scots Church, Collins Street, Melbourne, which began in 1940 and continued for the next 18 years.

His ministry had brought not only considerable fame but, from the royalties on the books, considerable income. Over a million books had sold at this stage. About the time he began the services at Scots, the Doctor and Mrs. Boreham therefore offered what in today's terms, would be about $15,000 to the Australian Baptist Missionary Society to establish a dispensary at Birisiri, in India, and to contribute a similar amount for the next five years towards its support. The benefaction was to remain anonymous and be called the Broadbanks Dispensary. But readers of Boreham's books may have wondered if it was only a coincidence that the dispensary should bear the same name as a character named John Broadbanks whom F. W. Boreham had made famous in his pages for many years. From now on all remuneration from his preaching passed on to the A.B.M.S. towards maintenance of the dispensary.

A second world preaching tour followed in 1936 even more successful, if we may use that term, than the one in 1928.

But for all the crowds who followed Boreham's preaching appearance whether at home or abroad, he was essentially a lonely man. His close ties to his study desk, meeting the demands for the output of his pen—he did not use a typewriter—left him little time to socialize, although he was an ardent cricket fan and a member of the Melbourne Cricket Club. He was not one to stand about after meetings just chatting with people nor was he ever seen to hurry. His colossal memory for names and faces served him well, and he seldom forgot anyone he had any dealings with.

Coinciding with the publication of his new book, *Dreams at Sunset* in 1954 came the announcement that, among the birthday honors, Queen Elizabeth II had conferred on Frank William Boreham the Order of Officer of the British Empire. His reaction was expressed in a letter to the author of this tribute, in reply to congratulations, "I appreciate the honor for its own sake, and especially for the sake of the citation, 'In recognition of his distinguished services to religion and literature as preacher and essayist.' It seems to show that I have kept first things first—always a matter of concern to me."

After his death on May 18, 1959, aged 88, a grateful denomination perpetuated his name by establishing the F. W. Boreham Hospital at Canterbury.

The Doctor was a "polished" individual, and although truly Australian, never lost his Englishness. Whether his style of preaching would appeal to today's generation with its casual approach to worship is a moot point, for he was a man of his time.

Nevertheless, the past few years have brought a revival of interest in the man and his ministry, numerous articles on his life and appreciations of his books have appeared in magazines around the world. Most of his books, however, have become collectors' items. Perhaps that fact may answer the question, "Is Boreham relevant to this vastly different age?"

A BOX OF BLOCKS

I

We had a birthday at our house today, and among the presents was a beautiful box of blocks. Each block represented
one of the letters of the alphabet. As I saw them being
arranged and rearranged upon the table, I started thinking.
For the alphabet has, in our time, come to its own. We go
through life muttering an interminable and incomprehensible jargon of initials. We tack initials on to our names—
before and after—and we like to see every one of them in
its place. As soon as I open my eyes in the morning, the
postman hands me a medley of circulars, postcards, and letters. One of them bids me to attend the annual meeting of
the S.P.C.A.; another reminds me of the monthly committee
meeting of the M.C.M.; a third asks me to deliver an address
at the P.S.A. In the afternoon I rush from an appointment at
the Y.M.C.A. to speak on behalf of the W.C.T.U.; and then,

having dropped in to pay my insurance premium at the A.M.P., I take the tram at the G.P.O., and ask the conductor to drop me at the A.B.C. I have accepted an invitation to a pleasant little function there—an invitation that is clearly marked R.S.V.P. And so on. There is no end to it. Life may be defined as a small amount of activity entirely surrounded by the letters of the alphabet.

Now the alphabet has a symbolism of its own. The man who coined the phrase '*as simple as A.B.C.*' went mad; he went mad before he coined it. There are, it is true, a few simplicities sprinkled among the intricacies of this old world of ours; but the alphabet is not one of them. I protest that it is most unfair to call the alphabet simple. Nobody likes to be thought simple nowadays; see how frantically we preachers struggle to avoid any suspicion of the kind! Any person living would rather be called a sinner—or even a saint—than a simpleton. Why, then, affront the alphabet, which, as we have seen, is working a prodigious amount of overtime in our service, by applying to it so very opprobrious an epithet?

'*As simple as A.B.C.,*' indeed! Macaulay's schoolboy may not have been as omniscient as the historian would lead us to believe but he at least knew that there is nothing simple about the A.B.C. The alphabet is the hardest lesson that a child is called upon to learn. Latin roots, algebraic equations, and the *Pons Asinorum* are mere nothings in comparison. Grown-ups have short memories. They forget the stupendous difficulties that they surmounted in their earliest infancy; and their forgetfulness renders them pitiless and unsympathetic. Few of us recognize the strain in which a child's brain is involved when, for the first time, he confronts the alphabet. The whole thing is so arbitrary; there is no clue. In his noble essay on *The Evolution of Language*, Professor Henry Drummond shows that the alphabet is really a picture-gallery. 'First,' he says, 'there was the onomatopoetic writing, the ideograph, the imitation of the actual object. This is the form we find in the Egyptian hieroglyphic. For a man a man is drawn, for a camel a camel, for a hut a hut. Then, to save time, the objects were drawn in shorthand—a couple of dashes for the limbs and one across, as in the Chinese, for a man; a square in the same language for a field; two strokes at an obtuse angle, suggesting the roof, for a house. To express further qualities, these abbreviated pictures were next compounded in ingenious ways. A man and a field together conveyed the idea of wealth; a roof and a woman represented home; and so on.' And thus, little by little, our letters were evolved. But the pictures have become so truncated, abbreviated, and emasculated, in the course of this evolutionary process, that a child, though notoriously fond of pictures, sees nothing fascinating in the letters of the alphabet. There is absolutely nothing about the first to suggest the sound A; nothing about the second to suggest the sound B. The whole thing is so incomprehensible; how can he ever hope to master it? An adult brain, introduced to such a conglomeration for the first time, would reel and stagger; is it any wonder that these childish cheeks get flushed or that the curly head turns at times very feverishly upon the pillow?

The sequence, too, is as baffling as the symbols. There is every reason why *two* should come between *one* and *three;* and that reason is so obvious that the tiniest tot in the class can appreciate it. But why must B come between A and C?

There is no natural advance, as in the case of the numerals. The letter B is not a little more than the letter A, nor a little less than the letter C. Except through the operation of the law of association, which only weaves its spell with the passing of the years, there is nothing about A to suggest B, and nothing about B to suggest C. The combination is a rope of sand. Robert Moffat only realized the insuperable character of this difficulty when he attempted to teach the natives of Bechuanaland the English alphabet. Each of his dusky pupils brought to the task an observation that had been trained in the wilds, a brain that had been developed by the years, and an intelligence that had been matured by experience. They were not babies. Yet the alphabet proved too much for them. Why should A be A? and why should B be B? and why should the one follow the other? Mr. Moffat was on the point of abandoning his educational enterprise as hopeless, when one thick-lipped and woolly-headed genius suggested that he should teach them to sing it! At first blush the notion seemed preposterous. There are some things which, like Magna Charta and minute-books, cannot be set to music. Robert Moffat, however, was a Scotsman. The tune most familiar to his childhood came singing itself over and over in his brain; by the most freakish and fantastic conjunction of ideas it associated itself with the problem that was baffling him; and, before that day's sun had set, he had his Bechuana pupils roaring the alphabet to the tune of *Auld Lang Syne!*

So ABC

D E F G

H I J K L M

NOPQ

RSTU

VWXYZ

The rhyme and meter fitted perfectly. The natives were so delighted that they strolled about the village shouting the new song at the tops of their voices; and Mr. Moffat declares that daylight was stealing through his bedroom window before the weird unearthly yells at last subsided. I have often wondered whether, in a more civilized environment, any attempt has been made to impress the letters upon the mind in the same way.

II

The symbolism of the alphabet rises to a sudden grandeur, however, when it is enlisted in the service of revelation. Long, long ago a startled shepherd was ordered to visit the court of the mightiest of earthly potentates, and to address him on matters of state in the name of the Most High. *'And the Lord said unto Moses, Come now, therefore, and I will send thee unto Pharaoh, and I will send thee also unto the children of Israel. And Moses said unto God, Behold, when I am come unto them and shall say, The God of your fathers hath sent me unto you, and they shall say, What is His name? What shall I say unto them? And God said unto Moses, Thus shalt thou say unto the children of Israel, I AM hath sent me unto you.'*

'*I am*—!'

'*I* am'—what?

For centuries and centuries that question stood unanswered; that sentence remained incomplete. It was a magnificent fragment. It stood like a monument that the sculptor had never lived to finish; like a poem that the poet, dying with his music in him, had left with its closing stanzas unsung. But the sculptor of *that* fragment was not dead; the singer of *that* song had not perished. For, behold, He lives for evermore! And, in the fullness of time, He reappeared and filled in the gap that had so long stood blank.

'*I am*—!'

'*I am*'—what?

'I am—*the Bread of Life!*' 'I am—*the Light of the World!*' 'I am—*the Door!*' 'I am—*the True Vine!*' 'I am—*the Good Shepherd!*' 'I am—*the Way, the Truth, and the Life!*' 'I am—*the Resurrection and the Life!*'

And when I come to the end of the Bible, to the last book of all, I find the series supplemented and completed.

'I am—*Alpha and Omega!*' 'I am—*A and Z!*' 'I am—*the Alphabet!*' The symbolism of which I have spoken can rise to no greater height than that. What, I wonder, can such symbolism symbolize? I take these birthday blocks that came to our house today and strew the letters on my study floor. So far as any spiritual significance is concerned, they seem as dead as the dry bones in Ezekiel's Valley. And yet '*I am the Alphabet!*' 'Come,' I cry, with the prophet of the captivity, 'come from the *Four Winds,* O Breath, and breathe upon these slain that they may live!' And the prayer has scarcely escaped my lips when lo, all the letters of the alphabet shine with a wondrous luster and glow with a profound significance.

III

For see, the *North* Wind breathes upon these letters on the floor, and I see at once that they are symbols of the *Inexhaustibility of Jesus!* '*I am Alpha and Omega!*' '*I am the Alphabet!*' I have sometimes stood in one of our great public libraries. I have surveyed with astonishment the serried ranks of English literature. I have looked up, and, in tier above tier, gallery above gallery, shelf above shelf, the books climbed to the very roof, while, looking before me and behind me, they stretched as far as I could see. The catalog containing the bare names of the books ran into several volumes. And yet the whole of this literature consists of these twenty-six letters on the floor arranged and rearranged in kaleidoscopic variety of juxtaposition. Which, I ask myself, is the greater—the literature or the alphabet? And I see at once that the alphabet is the greater because it is so inexhaustible. Literature is in its infancy. We shall produce greater poets than Shakespeare, greater novelists than Dickens, greater philosophers, historians, and humorists than any who have yet written. But they will draw upon the alphabet for every letter of every syllable of every word that they write. They may multiply our literature a million-million-fold; yet the alphabet will be as far from exhaustion when the last page is finished as it was before the first writer seized a pen.

'*I am—the Alphabet!*' He says. He means that He cannot be exhausted.

> For the love of God is broader
> Than the measures of Man's mind;
> And the heart of the Eternal
> Is most wonderfully kind.

The ages may draw upon His grace; the people of every nation and kindred and people and tongue—a multitude that no statistician can number—may kneel in contrition

at His feet; His love is as great as His power and knows
neither measure nor end. He is inexhaustible.

IV

And when the *South* Wind breathes upon these letters on the
floor, I see at once that they are symbols of the *Indispensability of Jesus*. Literature, with all its hoarded wealth, is as inac-
cessible as the diamonds of the moon until I have mastered
the alphabet. The alphabet is the golden key that unlocks to
me all its treasures of knowledge, poetry, and romance.

'*I am the Alphabet!*' He says; and He says it three separate times. For the words occur thrice in the Apocalypse. In
the *first* case they refer to the unfolding of the divine revelation; in the *second* they refer to the interpretation of historic experience; and in the *third* they refer to the unveiled
drama of the future. As the disciples discovered on the road
to Emmaus, I cannot understand my Bible unless I take
Him as being the key to it all; I cannot understand the
processes of historical development until I have given Him
the central place; I cannot anticipate with equanimity the
unfoldings of the days to come until I have seen the keys of
the eternities swinging at His girdle.

The alphabet is, essentially, an individual affair. In
order to read a single sentence, I must learn it *for myself.*
My father's intimacy with the alphabet does not help me to
enjoy the volumes on my shelves. The alphabet is indispensable *to me;* and so is He! There is something very pathetic
and very instructive about the story that Leigh Richmond
tells of *The Young Cottager.* 'The rays of the morning star,'
Mr. Richmond says, 'were not so beautiful in my sight as

the spiritual luster of this young Christian's character.' She was very ill when he visited her for the last time. 'There was animation in her look—there was more—something like a foretaste of heaven seemed to be felt, and gave an inexpressible character of spiritual beauty, even in death.'

'Where is your hope, my child?' Mr. Richmond asked, in the course of that last conversation.

'Lifting up her finger,' he says, 'she pointed to heaven, and then directed the same finger downward to her own heart, saying successively as she did so, "*Christ there!*" and "*Christ here!*" These words, accompanied by the action, spoke her meaning more solemnly than can easily be conceived.'

In life and in death He is our one indispensability. In relation to this world, and in relation to the world that is to come, He stands to the soul as the alphabet stands in relation to literature.

V

And when the *East* Wind breathes upon these letters on the floor, I see at once that they are symbols of the *Invincibility of Jesus*. '*I am—A and Z!*' He is at the beginning, that is to say, and He goes right through to the end. There is nothing in the alphabet before A; there is nothing after Z. However far back your evolutionary interpretation of the universe may place the beginning of things, you will find Him there. However remote your interpretation of prophecy may make the end of things, you will find Him there. He goes right through. The story of the ages—past, present, and future—may be told in a sentence 'Christ first, Christ last, and nought between but Christ.' Having begun, He completes. He is the Author and Finisher of our faith. He sets His face like a flint. Nothing daunts, deters, or dismays Him. 'I am confident,' Paul says, 'of this very thing, that He which hath begun a good work in you will perform it unto the end.' He never halts at H or L or P or X; He goes right through to Z. He never gives up.

VI

But the greatest comfort of all comes to me on the Wings, of the *West* Wind. For, when the West Wind breathes upon these letters on the floor, I see at once that they are symbols of the *Adaptability of Jesus.* The lover takes these twenty-six letters and makes them the vehicle for the expression of his passion; the poet transforms them into a song that shall be sung for centuries; the judge turns them into a sentence of death. In the hands of each they mold themselves to his necessity. The alphabet is the most fluid, the most accommodating, the most plastic, the most adaptable contrivance on the planet. Just because, in common with every person breathing, I possess a distinctive individuality, I sometimes feel as no person ever felt before, and I express myself in language such as no person ever used. And the beauty of the alphabet is that it adapts itself to my individual need. And that is precisely the beauty of Jesus. '*I am—the Alphabet!*' I may not have sinned more than others; but I have sinned differently. The experiences of others never sound convincing; they do not quite reflect my case. But, like the alphabet, He adapts Himself to *every* case. He is the very Savior I need.

F. W. Boreham, "A Box of Blocks," *Rubble and Roseleaves* (London: The Epworth Press, 1923), 236-248.

THE SQUIRREL'S DREAM

At the Melbourne Art Gallery this afternoon my attention was captivated and monopolized by a noble painting by the late John Pettie, R.A. It is entitled *Challenged,* and once adorned the walls of the Royal Academy in London. A gay young aristocrat has been called from his sumptuous couch in the early morning by a challenge to a duel. There he stands, attired in his blue dressing gown, holding the momentous document in his hand. His old serving-man, who has delivered the missive to his master, is vanishing through the distant door; a sword reposes suggestively upon a chair. But the whole artistry of the picture is concentrated in the face. It is the face of a thoughtless, shallow, self-indulgent young man-about-town suddenly startled to gravity and something like nobleness. By means of that face, the artist has skillfully portrayed the fact that life becomes smitten with sudden grandeur the moment it is challenged by stupendous issues. Life and death confront this young lord, and he becomes a new man as he realizes their stately significance.

No man amounts to much until all his faculties have been challenged. There must come a moment when a trumpet-blast, a pistol-shot, a bugle-call stirs all his pulses. And, this being so, life takes good care that, sooner or later, we shall each find ourselves dared by some tremendous situation. Therein lies the secret of that thirst for adventure, which is the hallmark of humanity.

I was listening last night to Dr. Adrian Carter, the principal of Clarendon House. Dear old Dr. Carter—'Magna Charta' as the boys irreverently call him! I would not miss the old gentleman's Speech Day oration for a king's ransom. His very appearance is a sight for sore eyes. He looks for all the world like a reincarnation of Mr. Pickwick. Everything about him—his chubby face, his prominent glasses, his expansive waistcoat, and even his trick of keeping his left hand, when speaking in public, under his coat-tails and flicking those coat-tails to emphasize his crucial points—intensifies the similarity to Mr. Pickwick. In his Speech Day deliverances, Dr. Carter lays down the law in such a way that every sentence seems a crystallization of the ultimate wisdom. On the theme with which he is dealing, there appears to be nothing more to be said. And yet, on the way home, you often catch yourself wondering.

This year, in his Speech Day address, the little old gentleman deplored the decay, in the rising generation, of the spirit of adventure. The world has been knocked into shape, he said, by people who scorned comfort and courted hardship. Anybody, he declared, flicking his coat-tails with special energy, anybody can follow the line of least resistance; anybody can settle down to the first job that comes; anybody can hug the coast. 'I trust,' he impressively observed in conclusion, 'I trust that the boys of Clarendon House will seek life's distant and more difficult tasks and thus maintain the most splendid traditions of the glorious past!' He resumed his seat, I need scarcely say, amidst a storm of tumultuous applause.

This is excellent—as far as it goes; the only trouble is that it does not carry us very far. For, to begin with, it is evident that it is some little time since the doctor himself was a boy. He has forgotten one or two things pertaining to his boyhood. For, in point of fact, no boy needs to have revived within him the spirit of adventure. It pulses in his blood all the time. No boy could have presented to the world a less adventurous appearance than did I. I do not recall one solitary occasion on which I became involved in censure through any daring escapade such as those of which the writers of schoolboy stories love to tell. To my parents and teachers my life must have appeared utterly placid, utterly tranquil, utterly commonplace. Yet, looking back, I can see that, all unsuspected, the spirit of adventure was throbbing within me. The worst crime ever laid to my charge was the crime of being absent-minded. The headmaster stigmatized me as 'an incorrigible wool-gatherer.' I distinctly remember a certain Examination Day. We had been told overnight that the Inspector was coming. We were to arrive at school next morning in our best Sunday clothes, with clean collar, brightly polished boots and finger-nails destitute of any funereal suggestion.

All went well until the Inspector tested our class in matters of geography. He asked some question about

Western Canada which sent my mind hurtling off on eventful journeys of its own. All at once, the boy sitting next me, giving me a dig with his elbow that almost fractured my ribs, whispered 'Java.' I then realized to my dismay that the Inspector was looking straight at me. Taking my school-fellow's violent but well-intentioned hint, I shot up my hand and said 'Java!'

'Exactly,' the great man replied with a patronizing smile, 'and now perhaps you will repeat the question that I asked you!'

I was floored, for the question had completely eluded me. His previous inquiry concerning Western Canada had dispatched my mind on a personally-conducted tour to the Rocky Mountains, and I was in the midst of a titanic struggle with a grizzly bear at the very moment at which he asked his further question relating to Java. Reviewing my boyhood, I can see that this sort of thing happened frequently. My unimaginative teachers obstinately insisted on asking their most ridiculous questions concerning Latin conjugations and recurring decimals at exciting moments when I was engaged in snatching a beautiful girl from the horns of an angry bull, or pursuing, single-handed, a powerful tribe of Iroquois Indians, or delivering a charming princess from a blazing palace or winning the Victoria Cross under circumstances of unprecedented gallantry.

The doctor was anxious, he said, to awaken in his boys the spirit of adventure. Has it never occurred to him, I wonder, that, in itself, the spirit of adventure is a pitifully poor thing? Two of the best books ever written—books that all the boys at Clarendon House will read before they are many days older—were written to show that, in itself, the spirit of adventure is worthless and even dangerous. It only becomes sublime when consecrated by a noble aim.

In the early pages of *Hereward the Wake*, Kingsley describes his hero as he first becomes conscious of his insatiable craving for adventure. Longing for a hectic and perilous career, he looks this way and that way in search of some opportunity of performing desperate and doughty deeds. He wearies of the humdrum of home. Out in the wide, wide world, beyond the borders of the too-familiar Bruneswald, he fancies that every hill and valley is swarming with dragons, giants, dwarfs, ogres, satyrs and similar weird and fantastic creatures. Where shall he go? To Brittany where, in the depths of the forest, beautiful fairies may be seen bathing in the fountains, and possibly be won and wedded by a sufficiently bold and dexterous knight? To Ireland, and marry some beautiful princess with gray eyes and raven locks and saffron smock and enormous bracelets made from the gold of her own native hills? No, he will go to the Orkneys and join Bruce and Ranald and the Vikings of the northern seas! Or he will go up the Baltic and fight the Letts upon the water and slay the bisons on the land! Or he will go South; see the magicians of Cordova and Seville; beard the Mussulman outside his mosque and perhaps bring home an Emir's daughter! Or he will go to the East, join the Varanger Guard, and, after being thrown to the lion for carrying off a fair Greek lady, will tear out the monster's tongue with his own hands and show the Orient what an Englishman is made of! At this stage, it will be observed, Hereward is seeking adventure for its own sake. The purpose of the exploit may be admirable or execrable:

it does not matter. It may leave him a hero or a cut-throat: he does not care.

Happily, Hereward discovered, comparatively early in his career, that a deed can only derive its luster from its motive and its aim. No deed, however audacious, is worth while unless it relieves the oppressed, raises the fallen, and makes the world a better place for everybody. This discovery represents the spiritual development of Kingsley's massive hero; and it is to trace this subtle evolution in Hereward's character that Kingsley wrote the book.

Pretty much the same may be said of *Don Quixote*. Cervantes saw to his sorrow that chivalry was running wild. The stories told by the men who were returning from the wars were inflaming the imagination of the youth of Castile to a positively dangerous degree. Hot-headed young enthusiasts were swept off their feet by an insatiable desire to cover themselves with glory. They would fight something or somebody, whether that something or somebody needed to be fought or not. Cervantes wrote his book to show that it is better to stay at home breaking stones by the roadside than to rush forth and hazard one's life in tilting at windmills.

It is not enough, therefore, to urge boys to develop the spirit of adventure. The spirit of adventure, undirected and unconsecrated, made Hereward the Wake a ruffian, made Don Quixote a clown; and has made many a boy a criminal. Dr. Carter must go one step further.

He must show that, provision having been made in the eternal scheme of things for the gratification of every legitimate appetite, provision has been made to gratify the thirst for adventure. In a quaint, fantastic and vivacious little play entitled *The Squirrel's Cage,* Tyrone Guthrie has demonstrated that each of us is like a squirrel shut up in a twirling prison. The very globe on which we live revolves continually. The year follows the same law: spring, summer, autumn, winter: the cycle goes round and round and round. A babe is born, a child develops, a youth matures, a man marries, a babe is born; and so the circle is again completed. Within this revolving cage it is natural that everything should tend towards monotony. All things go round and round and round!

Now, if I had been writing Tyrone Guthrie's play, I should have pointed out that, just beside the whirling cage, there is a small box-like compartment in which the squirrel sleeps. The little creature's antics in the open may be wonderfully spectacular; but, to me, his dreams in the sleeping compartment are much more enticing. Curled up there, he dreams—dreams every night the same dream—a dream of felicities that might have been. It is a dream of the vast woods, the swaying tree-tops, the arching boughs that look like bridges specially constructed to make easy a squirrel's progress from one end of the forest to the other. It is a dream of rich clusters of tawny filberts, of the greensward littered with beechnuts, of oak trees twinkling with innumerable acorns, and of a wondrous abundance of sweet forest seeds. It is a dream of a cozy little nest, lined with fur and fiber and leaves and moss, high up in the fork of the fir tree; it is a dream of the sweetest, shyest, daintiest little squirrel that ever hid coyly behind the bole of an elm tree; and of four tiny wee squirrels, scarcely to be recognized as squirrels, nosing and jostling each other in the secrecy of the quiet nest. But when he gets to this part of his dream the sleeper wakes up with a quiver and a start, stretches himself, passes out into the revolving cage, and, partly in sheer desperation, partly to throw off the memory of his dream, and partly to make himself believe that he is racing madly about the forest, he twirls his treadmill like a thing bewitched. Lookers-on laugh when they see him doing it: but he himself is not laughing. He has come back to the monotony of his treadmill after his dream of a wonderful and romantic escape.

The whole point of Tyrone Guthrie's play is that, at least once in every squirrel's life, the cage door is left open. And everything depends upon his behavior in that critical hour. Will he dare to pass out into the world to enjoy the actual realization of his dreams? Will his adventurous visions crystallize at last into actual experience? Or will he tremble in the presence of the unknown, and, terrified, creep back into his cage once more? That hour is the hour of his challenge; the greatest epoch in his life. Such a challenge comes, at some time and in some form, to each of us. We are presented with a sensational opportunity of escape. As a rule, when that sublime opportunity comes, we shrink from the unknown, hug the familiar cage, and allow the door to shut us in again. Tyrone Guthrie's hero, Henry Wilson, had the chance, in early youth, of going out to Africa. It appealed to all the adventurous instincts that tingled through his frame. But, on second thoughts, he felt that the exploit was extremely risky; his father pointed out the assured comforts that would accrue from his succeeding to the business; and so Henry, letting the cage-door close, went off to town every morning by the 9:23 and returned by the 6:13. Round and round and round!

The Church's evangel presents people with the most sublime of all those challenges. In his *Everlasting Man,* Mr. Chesterton says that life is a great game of Noughts and Crosses. The Nought—the circle—represents the basic monotony of life. Like the squirrel's cage, it goes round and round and round. Oriental religions, Mr. Chesterton points out, became infected by the dreariness of this fundamental monotony. The most typical and most eloquent symbol on an Eastern temple is a serpent with its tail in its mouth—a complete circle—a round that ends where it begins—a grind, a routine, a treadmill.

But beside the Nought, Mr. Chesterton says, stands the Cross. And, to play the game rightly, you must put the Cross inside the Nought. The four extremities of the Cross will pierce the Nought at four separate points, and, by the Cross, the monotony of life will be shattered into fragments and shattered for ever.

It is a perfect parable, needing neither elaboration nor application. But, having begun with a famous painting, I will close with another. Just two hundred years ago, Stenburg at Dusseldorf painted his *Gipsy Girl.* As his model posed upon the dais, her black eyes wandered round the studio. They were arrested by an altar-piece painted for Father Hugo of the Church of St. Jerome—a representation of the thorn-crowned face of Jesus. When the gipsy stepped down from her platform, she begged the artist to explain the picture to her. He tried, but found it difficult; for the thought of Christ stirred no profound emotion within him. When he had finished, the girl remarked simply: 'You must love Him very much, Signor, when He has done all that for you!'

The artless words pierced the painter's soul. They filled him with shame, for, in point of fact, he did not love Christ at all. But he soon did. And, when he did, he painted another picture—a picture of the Christ he now adored. Underneath the thorn-crowned face on the new canvas he inscribed the words:

All this I did for thee;
What hast thou done for Me?

He then presented it to the public gallery at Dusseldorf. And one day Count Zinzendorf was among the visitors who stood before it. Young, rich, gay and impressionable, the picture powerfully appealed to him, while the question beneath it rang through his soul like a challenge. It *was* a challenge, and he accepted it. He went out to serve his Savior. He became the founder of Moravian Missions. Within a few months missionaries were sent to the Esquimaux and to the people of the West Indies. In a year or two, evangelists of the Cross were dispatched to all parts of the world. The Moravian Brethren became, in 1738, the means of the conversion of John Wesley, and thus the amazing revival of the eighteenth century was initiated. The Cross had shattered the indolent monotony of Zinzendorf's life. He became a new man; the Church became a new Church; the world became a new world! The soul-stirring challenge had been accepted: the great escape had been made: and, as long as the world endures, people will rejoice in the sensational developments that followed.

F. W. Boreham, "The Squirrel's Dream," *A Witch's Brewing* (London: The Epworth Press, 1932), 89-99.

MIND YOUR OWN
BUSINESS!

I

Nancy was evidently very much annoyed.

'I felt like telling him to *mind his own business*,' she said, as she poured her tale of woe into my sympathetic ear.

'And why didn't you?' I replied. 'It's the best advice you can give to anybody; it seems a pity to have deprived him of it. Besides, it's a text; and you can never do much harm by quoting Scripture on suitable occasions.'

'A text!' she exclaimed in astonishment.

'Why, yes; didn't you know?' I answered. 'I can see that it's time I preached a sermon on it. Paul wrote to the Thessalonians telling them, in so many words, to *mind their own business;* and Jesus, without using the actual phrase, gave the same counsel to Peter. I shall be in no difficulty, therefore, about a starting-point for my sermon, and, as to divisions, they come of their own accord—

'*Firstly,* I shall say, *every man has a business.*

'*Secondly,* I shall say, *every man must make it his business to attend to his business.*

'*Thirdly,* I shall say, *no man can satisfactorily look after another man's business.* He must mind his own.'

My rough-and-ready sermonizing had its inevitable effect upon Nancy. She did not exactly go to sleep, but she was manifestly soothed and mollified.

'Dear me,' she exclaimed, smilingly, as she reached for her umbrella and prepared to go, 'I had no idea that sermons were so quickly made!' And off she went.

But, as with most of the work that is done hastily and costlessly, nothing came of it. The sermon that I proposed to myself that evening, as I chatted with Nancy, has never been preached. I scarcely know why. The theme is important enough, in all conscience. The finest epitaph that could be graven upon any man's tomb would be the testimony: *HE KNEW HOW TO MIND HIS OWN BUSINESS.* And, even at the Day of Judgment, I doubt whether any man will receive nobler praise than that.

II

Unfortunately, we come into the world with our eyes shut and with our minds totally uninstructed. It is a cruel handicap. If our eyes were open, and if, before our advent, we had learned to read, we should notice that over the portals by which we enter there is an inscription. It reads: *NO ADMITTANCE EXCEPT ON BUSINESS.* We are none of us here for fun. We are none of us here to poke about. We are none of us here by chance. We are not sight-seers or

star-gazers. Each of us must make it his business to discover
the business with which he has been entrusted. 'It is a great
pity,' as Sir Thomas Smith, the Secretary to Queen Elizabeth, remarked on his deathbed, 'it is a great pity that men
know not to what end they are born into this world until
they are ready to go out of it!'

We are each endowed with individuality. Nancy is
Nancy, and Kate is Kate. Kate cannot do Nancy's work
in the world, and Nancy cannot do Kate's. Every man has
business of *his own*.

Dr. Alexander Whyte was fond of telling the story of
an old Puritan divine who, whenever he added a new book
to his library, wrote in it his name, William Perkins; and
then, underneath, the words 'Remember, thou art a Minister of the Word: *mind thy business.*' I wish Dr. Whyte had
told us a little more about good old William Perkins. One
of these days I mean to investigate the matter. I feel sure
that William Perkins was a most engaging and lovable character, highly esteemed by his people and greatly revered by
his brother-ministers. He was never indolent or lazy, for he
had his business to mind. On the other hand, he was never
restless or fidgety or neurasthenic in his lust of activity, for
he knew that the culture of his own soul is a most important part of a minister's business, and he was determined
to mind it. Nor was he meddlesome. He did not try to
mind the politician's business or the journalist's business or
the entertainer's business; but, with all his heart and soul,
he tried to mind *his own business*. And, although I know
nothing of his ministerial record, I feel sure that, in the
parish over which William Perkins was set, there were very
few souls that were not redeemed or rebuked, stimulated

or comforted, as a result of his quiet and helpful influence.
Like Goldsmith's village preacher, he was

> Prompt at every call,
> He watched and wept, he prayed and felt for all;
> And, as a bird each fond endearment tries,
> To tempt its new-fledged offspring to the skies,
> He tried each art, reproved each dull delay,
> Allured to brighter worlds, and led the way.

For *that*, he would have said, was *his* business, and he
was resolved to mind it.

III

From the fact that Jesus told Peter to *mind his own business* I
learn that life's greatest peril is the peril of distraction. It was
the most momentous and memorable day in Peter's career.
It was the day on which his great wrong was put right, as far
as a wrong can ever be put right in this world. He had three
times denied his Lord; and, to his delight, had been given
the opportunity of three times confessing Him: '*I love Thee*'
'*Thou knowest that I love Thee!*' '*Thou knowest all things;
Thou knowest that I love Thee!*' In response to that threefold
avowal, Peter had been entrusted with a sublime commis-
sion. One would have expected that, having received such
a charge from the divine lips, he would have gone apart to
ponder the greatness of the grace by which he had been
forgiven, and the glory of the ministry to which he had
been called. But, just at that moment, he caught sight of
John. '*Peter, seeing him, saith to Jesus, Lord, and what shall*

this man do?' And Jesus told him to *mind his own business.*
'*What is that to thee?*' He asked. '*Follow thou Me!*'

The least thing is apt to distract our attention from
our main business if we are not taking it very seriously. On
catching sight of John's face, Peter forgets all about his own
forgiveness and his reinstatement in the ministry; his mind
flies off at a tangent. What is to be *John's* mission in life? As
if *that* mattered to Peter! In his chapter on 'The Boar Hunt,'
in *Quentin Durward,* Sir Walter Scott shows how the life
of King Louis was jeopardized by the sudden division of
the pack into two parts. A young boar crossed the track of
the animal that the party was pursuing, and, instantly, all
the dogs, except the most experienced ones, set out on the
new trail. Many of the riders also followed this false scent.
But the king was too cunning a sportsman to be so easily
drawn aside. He knew that the original quarry was worried and exhausted, while the new scent was the scent of a
creature that was fresher than the horses and the hounds.
Louis held to the first trail, and was soon face to face with
the boar that he had so tenaciously pursued. And if the
young huntsmen and the young hounds had been equally
wise, he would not have been compelled to encounter in
solitude the infuriated beast. And had they declined to be
distracted, they would have shared the royal exultation at
the close of that memorable day. We should all taste the joy
of triumph more often if we adopted the king's method.
But, to our own undoing, we turn aside. Just as Peter gets
his first clear glimpse of his own life-work, he catches sight
of John. It is a small circumstance, but it is just enough
to cause his mind to swerve. '*And what shall this man do?*'

Peter's behavior called loudly for rebuke, and he received it.
Jesus told him to *mind his own business.*

IV

There is all the difference in the world between an *inquiring* mind and an *inquisitive* mind. The one is often the enemy of the other. Peter is anxious to know what part *he* can play in hastening the Kingdom of God: he is to be commended, he has an *inquiring* mind. Peter is curious to know what part *John* is to play: he is merely *inquisitive:* he must be told to *mind his own business.* This kind of thing is very common.

I had great hopes of Arthur Cunningham. He got into the way of attending the church: seemed impressed: and I had many conversations with him. Like Peter, he was anxious about himself—anxious to be right, anxious to be of service. But it all came to nothing. Just as everything was promising well with him, he allowed his mind to become involved in a multitude of abstract questions. His curiosity was aroused as to the mystery of the beginning of things. How was the universe fashioned and furnished? Were the worlds created or evolved? Were the 'days' of Genesis literal days or vast geologic ages? Now it is a fine thing for a young fellow to apply his mind to the stately and fascinating problems of the universe, just as it is a fine thing for Peter to interest himself in the future of his friend. But there is a time for everything. At that moment Peter's whole mind should have been focused on *his own* future; and, at the period of which I am thinking, Arthur Cunningham's mind should have been focused on his soul's salvation. It is no good shelving the question, *What must I do to be saved?* in order to investigate the latest theory of evolution. Like Peter, Arthur allowed an *inquisitive* mind to take the place of an *inquiring* mind. So did Effie Gray.

Effie became a member of my Young People's Class. One evening she remained behind to speak with me. She was thinking of joining the Church. I was delighted, and did all that I could to encourage her. Then, quite unaccountably, she cooled off. She not only said no more about joining the Church, but she absented herself quite frequently from the class.

'Well, Effie,' I said to her, one evening, 'we never have a talk about things nowadays!'

'No,' she replied, 'I have been studying a good deal.'

'Studying, Effie?' I replied. 'That's good. And what is it that you are studying?'

'Well,' she answered, a little diffidently, 'for awhile I made a study of spiritualism; but I couldn't make much of that; so then I took up the study of prophecy. I've read quite a lot of books and compared their diagrams and charts; but it's very confusing. I can't reconcile the teaching of the little horn in Daniel with the teaching of the seventh seal in Revelation.'

Poor Arthur! Poor Effie! They are finding that an *inquisitive* mind is a poor substitute for an *inquiring* mind. It is good to be interested, like Arthur, in the *beginning* of things; and it is good to be interested, like Effie, in the *end* of things; but, on the whole, it is better to leave the study of algebra until the multiplication table has been mastered. It is time for Peter to settle the affairs of John when *his own* relationship with his Lord has been clearly established and defined.

V

There is such a thing as *a sublime selfishness*. It is all very well for Peter to interest himself in John, but there are times when it is Peter's bounden duty to forget all about John and to concentrate all his attention on Peter. We are living in a world in which everybody knows what everybody else ought to do. We can each of us see at a glance what the Prime Minister ought to do, and what the Government ought to do, and what the Opposition ought to do, and what the editor ought to do. Peter always seems to know exactly what John ought to do. The pity of it is that we are not sufficiently self-centered. If only Peter would give his whole heart and soul to discovering what Peter ought to do! If only Peter would *mind his own business*.

No man can carry everybody's burden. The years teach us to leave a few worries for other people. Peter will go down to a premature grave if he persists in concerning himself so much with the business of the other disciples. Like Towser, most of us wear ourselves out by dissipating our energies. Everybody knows of Towser.

'The poor dog is tired out,' said Mary, as the farm wagon drove into the yard, and Towser, covered with the dust of the road, dropped lolling and panting upon the grass.

''Tisn't the journey he had to take that tired him,' laughed the farmer. 'He's used himself up by zigzagging from one side of the road to the other, and 'tendin' to everything that didn't concern him. He couldn't pass a gate without running through it, to see what was on the other side, nor see a hen anywhere along the road without feelin' called upon to chase her. Every dog that barked started him to barkin', and everything that moved took him out of his way to find out what it was, and where it was goin'. No wonder he's tired!'

No wonder, indeed! We should all be a little less weary at the end of the day, and we should all live a little longer and a little more pleasantly, if we were just a little more self-centered. Few of us know how to *mind our own business.*

Happily, the discipline of life tends to turn our eyes inward. There was a time, many years ago, when I greatly disliked one of Charles Wesley's hymns and declined to sing it. It seemed to me so shockingly self-centered, and I had not then learned that there is a virtue in certain forms of selfishness. The hymn begins:

A charge to keep I have,
A God to glorify,
A never-dying soul to save,
And fit it for the sky.

As the years have come and gone, however, I have become reconciled to the hymn. When we are in our teens faith seems wonderfully simple; but, as life advances, we discover that it is a much more complicated affair than we once supposed. For the salvation of one's own soul is a tremendous business.

So is the ministry to which Peter had just been called. When Peter shudders under the solemnity of the ordination charge, he is not likely to be inordinately curious as to the responsibilities of James and John. He feels that he has enough to think about. His work, as Doddridge sings, 'might fill an angel's heart, and filled the Savior's hands.' He will *mind his own business!*

VI

The beauty of it is that the man who *minds his own business* always finds his course perfectly clear. '*What is that to thee? Follow thou Me!*' said the Savior.

'*Follow thou Me!*' Could anything be more exquisitely simple? Could any instructions be more delightfully explicit? When life becomes a direct relationship between Himself and myself, it is wonderful how plain my path appears.

F. W. Boreham, "Mind Your Own Business!," *A Tuft of Comet's Hair* (London: The Epworth Press, 1926), 230-240.

THE EAGLE'S NEST

I

The scramble that led us to the eagle's nest was, I think, the stiffest proposition of the kind that I have ever tackled. My whole body was one great ache for days afterwards. The dew was sparkling on the grass when we started, and rabbits were scurrying in all directions. The bush orchids were at their best, and the slopes were delicately draped in wild flowers. The song of the birds was at times almost deafening. As we passed through a belt of bush, a squirrel leapt from tree to tree beside us, and then, greatly daring, descended and skipped along in front. Every now and again he would turn cheekily round; sit facing us, with his tail gracefully curled behind him; wait until we were within a yard or two of him; and then go prancing on ahead once more. At the fringe of the bush he vanished, however, and, except for a fox that stole out from behind a huge boulder and crept stealthily down into the fern, we saw no other living creature in the course of our climb. The eagles have the heights pretty much to themselves. All the other birds and beasts prefer the lower levels.

We rested for lunch on a ledge of rock that commanded an enchanting view of the plains that we had left. The world seemed spread out at our feet. It was a glorious panorama. And, save when we broke the stillness with our voices, the silence was almost oppressive. Not a sound was to be heard. The barking of dogs, the singing of birds, and even the chirping of insects were left behind us. Such sound belonged to the world far below.

The first indication that we were approaching something unusual was the atrocious smell. It grew worse and worse with every step that we took, becoming at last well-nigh insufferable. By this time, too, we began to notice, strewn in the long grass around us, the bleached bones of all sorts of animals and birds. The place was a perfect charnel-house. Then, drawing nearer to the precipice, our eyes were offended by the ghastly remains of various creatures in all stages of decomposition and decay. Here was half a rabbit; there was a hare so mutilated as to be scarcely recognizable; and over yonder the head and shoulders of air opossum, the hind-quarters of a bandicoot, an iguana horribly mangled, and some young grouse that the bigger birds had torn to tatters. The hillside was a grim and noisome shambles.

We lay down, craned over, and, in a huge recess on the shelf of rock below us, we saw the home of the eagles. It had evidently been there for many years; and, each year, substantial additions had been made to it. It seemed to us that wagon-loads of material must have been woven into its construction. It was an immense affair, lined and made comfortable with fern and grass and feathers. Three eaglets—ugly little things with bristles like porcupines and beaks that seemed many sizes too large—jostled each other in the shadowy hollow of their rocky home. We watched them curiously for a moment; but only for a moment. The longer we stayed, the more overpowering the situation became. The whole shelf round the nest was littered with gruesome offal from which a thick steam and a hideous stench were rising. We turned away disgusted yet delighted. Glad as we were to have seen the nest, we were no less thankful to have left it.

II

It was Moses who, in his majestic swan song, unfolded the *Parable of the Eagle's Nest.* Amid the most fearsome and awe-inspiring scenery, he was about to die. The landscape was a wilderness of splintered peaks, jagged summits, scarped crags, and beetling cliffs. Everything was wild, weird, precipitous, desolate, and grand. Moses reflected that the people were confronted by a hurricane of change. They were passing from one land to another; they were passing from one leadership to another; and they were passing from a life that was wild, restless, and nomadic to a life that was settled, agricultural, and domestic. In view of this whirl of transition, Moses gave them a Philosophy of Disturbances. Employing an image suggested by the great birds soaring in the skies above him—the birds that had their nests amid those solitary fastnesses and gloomy ravines—he tells them that, *as an eagle stirreth up her nest, fluttereth over her young, spreadeth abroad her wings, taketh them, beareth them on her wings,* so Jehovah had dealt with them. With the memory of my visit to the eagle's nest fresh in my mind, the picture did not at first attract me. An eagle's nest with its hideous surroundings makes up a picture that is by no means pleasant. But the Bible has a wonderful way of making sordid things sublime. Objects in themselves unlovely become the vehicles by which the most graceful and priceless truths are conveyed. The prodigal sitting beside his swine, tearing ravenously at their husks, is by no means a delectable conception; yet we would sacrifice half the poetry of the ages rather than have that gem torn from us. Let us take a second glance at the eagle's nest! The eagle's nest, Moses declares, is a revelation! Not only so, it is a revelation of God: *As the eagle so the Lord.* What, I wonder, does it reveal?

III

It is a revelation of the *God who Builds.* For, now that I come to think again, I am impressed by the fact that that immense nest among the crags has about it some very arresting qualities. It is, after all, a striking spectacle. The eyrie is so skillfully chosen! The spot is so secluded, so strong, so safe! And how stoutly the foundations are laid! How cunningly branch is laid upon branch, stick dovetailed into stick, twig woven into twig! All the essential principles of engineering receive exemplification here. What architects and what builders these great birds are!

So the Lord, says Moses. *As the eagle so the Lord.* He maintains that the eagles are but the symbols of God by whom they were taught their craft.

The God who Builds *the Nations!* And no nation that failed to recognize His handiwork in its construction ever yet came to anything worth mentioning. Take our own! Of all people on the face of the earth we should most richly deserve to pass out into the night of oblivion and forgetfulness if we failed to recognize a divine hand in the shaping of our destinies. The *History of England* is, far and away, the greatest romance that has ever been written. There is nothing in legend or fable to compare with it. In the old days, in the absence of history, Englishmen wove for themselves pretty fancies like the story of King Arthur and the Knights of the Round Table. Since then the stately drama of history has been enacted. The stories of Norman and Saxon, of Roman and Dane, of Alfred and Edward, of Cromwell and Pitt, of 'the spacious days of great Elizabeth' and the record reign of Queen Victoria—such annals have eclipsed the luster of those earlier imaginings, and have outshone the dainty myths that the poets dreamed. The pageant is so impressive that we feel instinctively that the magnificent procession is being marshaled, that the evolution is an ordered and prearranged scheme, that there is an intelligence, a will, a heart behind it all. We discover God. As Rudyard Kipling sings:

> Fair is our land, oh, goodly is our heritage;
> Humble ye, my people, and be fearful in your mirth!
> For the Lord our God most High, He hath made this
>   deep as dry,
> He hath smote for us this pathway to the ends of all
>   the earth!

The God who Builds *the Churches!* Who can read the story of the Church—her foundation, her struggles, her sufferings, her triumphs—without feeling that the Church is a divine creation? Who can sing:

> I love Thy Church, O God
> Her walls before Thee stand,
> Dear as the apple of Thine eye,
> And graven on Thy hand,

without giving thanks for all that the Church has meant to people?

The God who Builds *our Homes!* Round the dome of the Eddystone Lighthouse is a text: *Except the Lord build the house, they labor in vain that build it!* In view of the history of the Eddystone Lighthouse that passage is very suggestive. But I confess that once upon a time the text puzzled me. *Except the Lord build the house, they labor in vain that build it!* Is that quite true? Is it not possible for a man, without asking the divine help, to build a house? It is: and the text does not deny that it is. It simply says that, building a house, he builds it *in vain.* For the house that he builds will never be anything but a *house.* And who wants to live in a *house?* We love to live in *homes.* And it is only by the magic touch of a divine hand that *houses* become *homes.* The heathen have no *homes,* says one of our most acute *philosophers:* they have but *houses!*

IV

It is a revelation of the *God who Breaks. As the eagle breaketh up her nest ... so the Lord.* If the eaglets are too comfortable, they will never attempt to fly. So the mother-bird tears out the soft lining of the nest and exposes their tender skin to the hard twigs underneath.

So the Lord, says Moses. There are divine disturbances. The old home breaks up; the parents die; the family is scattered. The church is invaded by change; ministers leave; members go this way and that way. Our comfort is rudely violated. Like the eaglets, we are put on our mettle and are compelled to fend for ourselves.

V

It is a revelation of the *God who Broods. As the eagle fluttereth over her young ... so the Lord.*

She hovers over the nest. She would have her eaglets to feel that if they try—and fail—she is close at hand to save them. She seeks to awaken desire and excite them to emulation. As they see the might of her wings, they may be tempted to try their own. That is the way of all young things. *So the Lord,* says Moses. He draws near to us and makes His presence felt. In Browning's words:

God glows above
With scarce an intervention, presses close,
And palpitatingly, His soul o'er ours.

And never does His presence press upon us but we feel as the eaglets feel. They look up at the hovering bird and long to be like her. We look up at the hovering Presence and long to be like Him. Therein lies the significance of the New Testament story—the sweetest story ever told. God came very near to Man; assumed his nature and wore his flesh; and He did it in order that Man, too much oppressed by his own impotence, might spread his feeble pinions and soar into the skies.

VI

It is a revelation of the *God who Bears*. *As the eagle beareth them on her wings so the Lord*. The eaglets spread their baby pinions at last—and fall into the abyss! But, with a rush and a swoop, the mother-bird plunges into the depth beneath them, and, catching them on her wings, bears them back to the nest on the shelf.

So the Lord, says Moses. Like the eagle, He bids us do what we have not strength to do in order that, in attempting it, we may acquire the strength to do it. Any fool can do what he *can* do: it takes a man of some faith to do what he *cannot* do. Yet it is by such men that nations are saved, for they are the salt of the earth. 'Always do what you are afraid to do!'

Emerson's aunt used to say to him; and, years afterwards, he declared that it was *high counsel*. The eaglet that whimpers *I can't!* dies on the rock and adds its carcass to the carrion already there. But the eaglets that attempt to fly when flight seems hopelessly impossible, soon find themselves lords of the blue. That is what Moses meant. The man who, in the daring of faith, undertakes what he cannot perform will soon astonish the world by performing it.

F. W. Boreham, "The Eagle's Nest," *The Three Half-Moons* (London: The Epworth Press, 1929), 185-193.

THE AGNOSTIC

I had occasion, on Thursday, to visit Brambleford. I took
the afternoon train, and nothing much happened until I
had been some hours on the way. The evening was cool and
pleasant. Dusk was just falling when the train stopped at
an up-country station. I instinctively glanced up and down
the platform to see who was about and what they were
doing. There is no business quite as fascinating as other
people's business. I soon forgot the train and everything else
in watching an old man and woman from out-back who
were welcoming, with evident emotion, a smartly-dressed
young fellow who stepped from a carriage near the engine.
Then my reverie was rudely disturbed. I became conscious
of a movement close at hand, and, turning my head, found
a little old gentleman, heavily laden with suitcase, rugs,
books, papers, umbrella, overcoat, and other odds and
ends, attempting to enter my own compartment. I opened
the door and assisted him with his luggage; and he bustled
into the corner immediately opposite me. The train was

soon in motion again and we quickly settled down to conversation. He was, it seemed, an officer of a church which I happened to know, and he was intimate with a number of people in whom I was particularly interested.

'You took me by surprise,' I said; 'I did not see you coming across the platform to the train.'

'I didn't,' he exclaimed, 'I came from the next compartment. There's a fellow in there reading the *Life of Huxley*. I began to talk to him and he told me that he's an agnostic himself. I couldn't stand that, you know, so I made up my mind to come to another compartment. I am very glad now that I did.'

I acknowledged the compliment and we spent a very pleasant hour together. Then, as the train slowed clown on approaching Willoughby Junction, I began to collect my belongings.

'Changing here?' my companion inquired.

'Oh, no,' I replied, 'but I'm going into the next compartment for awhile. The fact is, I have a weakness for any man who is fond of Huxley, and,' I added, mischievously, 'I'm a bit of an agnostic myself!'

In the next compartment I found a most agreeable and entertaining companion. We discussed Huxley for awhile, and then, after the fashion of such desultory conversations, we talked about everything under the sun.

'Our little friend,' he said, nodding towards the next compartment, 'was horrified when I told him I'm an agnostic. But, of course, when I say that I'm an agnostic, I mean that I'm an agnostic. Like Huxley, I simply do not know. I was brought up in Church and Sunday school; but I've been very hard hit since then. I lost my wife; then I lost

my money; and I've just been up to town to bury my only
child. Somehow, the easy-going faith of my boyhood has
fallen to pieces. It wouldn't stand the strain. And now I
don't know where I am; and I'm reading anything that will
bring me in touch with minds that have, at some time or
other, been similarly confused and bewildered.'

The sound of our voices—and the solitude of his own
compartment—proved too much for our little friend next
door. At Golden Creek he came bustling back with all his
goods and chattels, and the three of us whiled away very
happily the last stretch of our long journey.

II

Very tired, I reached my destination at about ten o'clock
that night, and went straight to bed. I quickly fell asleep
and dreamed a strange dream. I was, I thought, in the
pulpit; and, in glancing round upon the congregation, I
caught sight of my two traveling companions sitting side
by side in a pew not far from me. The conviction fastened
itself upon me that I must preach a sermon specially suited
to them both.

'Here, in my congregation, is an agnostic,' I said to
myself; 'and here, sitting beside him, is a man who is so sure
of his faith that he is horrified at the behavior of the other
in calling himself an agnostic. What text can I select, or
what subject can I take, that will meet the intellectual and
spiritual requirements of both men?'

The perturbation into which this problem threw me
was too much for my slumbering powers; and, still revolving the perplexing question, I awoke. But the puzzle did not

vanish with the dream from which it sprang. All through the morning, as I kept the appointments that had taken me to Brambleford, I found myself cogitating the subject-matter of my dream. I returned to town by the evening train. Neither of my former companions was to be seen. I had a compartment to myself. And, all the way, my mind insisted on wrestling with the query propounded in my dream. If, on the coming Sunday, I were called to preach to a congregation that included a number of agnostics, and a number of devout men and women whose faith was so serene that they had no patience with agnosticism, what subject should I take? And, as suddenly as it arose, the problem was solved!

For, like a flash of lightning, it occurred to me that the New Testament contains a story that seemed specially written to meet my singular requirements. Did not Paul preach one of his most striking and notable sermons standing beside an altar that had been reared by the Athenian agnostics, an altar that bore the inscription AGNOSTO THEO—To the Unknown God?

'Here,' I said to myself, 'is Agnosticism's special shrine!'

'And here, standing beside it,' I added, 'is the faith's most valiant exponent and defender!' And as I contemplated that twofold spectacle—the Altar and the Apostle— I felt that I had a theme entirely to my mind. It presented a powerful appeal, both to the agnostic and to the man who has no sympathy with agnosticism. I fervently wished that my dream could be realized and that both my traveling companions could be in my congregation on Sunday.

III

Every agnostic should find room, within the compass of his agnosticism, for an altar. That is the point that I should strive to impress upon the minds of the agnostics in my congregation. These Athenian agnostics did not know: their minds were shadowed with the gloom of a vast uncertainty: but they reared an altar to the God who was unknown to them: and they worshipped at that agnostic shrine until the unknown God sent His apostle to reveal to them the truth for which their hearts were aching. The man who cannot find the light must never put up the shutters. Let him keep his curtain drawn back, and his blinds well up, so that, when the dawn steals over the hills, he will catch the very first ray. The man who does not know cannot afford to be dogmatic or self-assertive. The sincere and genuine agnostic will never adopt a blatant attitude. He will be modest and even reverent. It will never seriously occur to him to argue that, because he does not know God, therefore there is no God. He will be more likely to imitate these Athenian agnostics and raise an altar to the God whom he does not know, wistfully hoping that the God to whom he rears his altar will somehow send him enlightenment and faith and hope.

My friend in the railway carriage was reading the *Life of Huxley;* and certainly Huxley—the greatest of all our agnostics—was reverent in his agnosticism. In the volume that my friend slipped into his suitcase as the train slowed at last into Brambleford station, he will find two very affecting episodes. Huxley came out to Australia: fell in love with a girl in Sydney who proved herself in every way worthy of him: but he had to wait many long years before he was in a position to invite her to go to England and become his bride. They were married at last, however, and the first of the two stories to which I have referred has to do with the birth of their boy. It is the last night of the Old Year, and, in a fever of concern, Huxley is waiting to hear that he is a father. He spends the anxious hour in framing a resolution. In his diary he pledges himself 'to smite all humbugs, however big; to give a nobler tone to science; to set an example of abstinence from petty personal controversies and of toleration for everything but lying; to be indifferent as to whether the work is recognized as mine or not, so long as it is done. It is half-past ten at night. Waiting for my child. I seem to fancy it the pledge that all these things shall be.' And the next entry runs:

'*New Year's Day, 1859.* Born five minutes before twelve. *Thank God!*'

Mark that '*Thank God!*' and then note what follows. Four years later, when the child is snatched from him, he makes another entry and then closes the journal for ever. He has no heart to keep a diary afterwards.

'Our Noel, our first-born, after being for nearly four years our delight and our joy, was carried off by scarlet fever in forty-eight hours. This day week he and I had a great romp together. On Friday his restless head, with its bright blue eyes and tangled golden hair, tossed all day upon the pillow. On Saturday night I carried his cold still body here into my study. Here, too, on Sunday night, came his mother and I to that holy leave-taking. My boy is gone; but, in a higher and better sense than was in my mind when, four years ago, I wrote what stands above, I feel that my fancy

has been fulfilled. I say heartily and without bitterness—
Amen, so let it be!'

'*Thank God!*' exclaims our great Agnostic when the
child is born.

'*Amen!*' he says, submissively, when the little one is
buried.

That *Thank God* and that *Amen* are extremely significant. They show that, like the agnostics of Athens, Huxley
found room for an altar within the compass of his agnosticism. I am very hopeful that my friend in the railway carriage will see the profound significance of that.

I shall make this point as impressive as I possibly can;
and then I shall turn to the people in my congregation who,
like the little old gentleman on the train, have scant sympathy with those whose faith is not as tranquil as their own.

IV

*For every Christian should find room, within the compass of
his faith, for a moderate amount of agnosticism.* That is why,
on leaving the little old gentleman in the one compartment
to join the man whom he had so intolerantly left in the
other, I assured him that I was a bit of an agnostic myself.
Every man should be.

Every Christian should be alarmed unless there are at
least a few vital and indispensable verities of which he is
absolutely certain. Paul lays his hand reverently and sympathetically on this agnostic altar; for Paul knows what it is
to be shadowed by uncertainty on certain points. But, for
all that, Paul cherishes in his heart a few serene and stupendous certainties. *We know,* he says, *we know* that all things

work together for good. *We know* whom we have believed. *We know* that if our earthly house were dissolved, we have a building of God, a house not made with hands, eternal in the heavens. This is magnificent. It is as it should be. Without some such basis of confidence, faith would wilt and shrivel and die.

But faith is incomplete, too, without its uncertainties. For, obviously, without uncertainties, faith would not be faith. There are things that I know and there are things that I do not know. I have said that every Christian should be alarmed unless there are a few things of which he is absolutely certain; but it is just as true that every Christian should be alarmed unless there are a few things of which he is sublimely ignorant. There are a thousand questions to which he can only reply: 'I do not know!' To that extent he is an agnostic, and his agnosticism is good. If his faith is so small that it can be contained within the compass of his intelligence it is not big enough to save his everlasting soul.

Every day of his life a man should thank God for his knowledge and for his ignorance—for the one as much as for the other. For ignorance is one of the luxuries of existence. Life will have a little snap and sparkle for us so long as we retain some small stock of ignorance; but, if that goes, the joy of living will come abruptly to an end and the curtain may as well fall. Ignorance has a truly heroic record. It was the ignorance of Columbus as to the lands beyond the sunset that led him to open the gates of a new hemisphere; it was the ignorance of Peary as to the character of the frozen North that led him to the discovery of the Pole; it was the ignorance of Scott and Amundsen and Mawson that drove them to wrest from the Antarctic its hoarded secrets; it was the ignorance of Livingstone as to the whereabouts of the fountains of Herodotus that led to the opening up of Africa and the abolition of the slave trade; it was the ignorance of men concerning the baffling problems of the universe that brought into being the splendid pageant of scientific discovery; it was the ignorance of medical men as to some way of healing the world's diseases that gave us the cures and ameliorations for which all mankind is grateful. The world has every reason to be glad of its ignorance; in that respect, as in so many others, it has much to be thankful for!

Blessed are the ignorant; blessed are the people who do not know; blessed are the agnostics! A little child is necessarily ignorant: his mind is a blank: he has not yet begun to learn. Yet, when we wish to describe the maximum of mortal bliss, we say that a man is as happy as a little child. A child is in a world of sensations: his ignorance makes every commonplace object an astonishment to him. For this reason, Macaulay says, in his essay on Milton, for this reason no man can become a great poet until he has recaptured the bliss of his childish ignorance. He must unlearn. The statement throws a flood of light upon those striking words in which Jesus affirmed that only by becoming a little child can any man enter the Kingdom of God. He must feel as a child feels when he gazes for the first time upon the stars; he must realize the incomprehensibility of the incomprehensible: he must find a large sediment of agnosticism mingling with the ingredients that compose his faith.

V

And the beauty of it all is that here, beside this Agnostic Altar, stands an Apostle! That strikes me as wonderfully suggestive. Let me but plant a tree outside my window, and, as sure as God is God, He will send a bird to sing to me from the leafy shade of its branches. Let me but rear an altar to the Unknown, and, as sure as God is God, He will send some apostolic messenger to dispel my ignorance and to reveal to my delighted eyes the unsearchable riches of Christ.

F. W. Boreham, "The Agnostic," *When the Swans Fly High* (London: The Epworth Press, 1931), 42-52.

CATHERINE BOOTH'S TEXT

I

Who that was in London on October 14, 1890, can forget the extraordinary scenes that marked the funeral of Catherine Booth? It was a day of universal grief. The whole nation mourned. For Mrs. Booth was one of the most striking personalities, and one of the mightiest spiritual forces, of the nineteenth century. To the piety of a Saint Teresa she added the passion of a Josephine Butler, the purposefulness of an Elizabeth Fry, and the practical sagacity of a Frances Willard. The greatest in the land revered her, trusted her, consulted her, deferred to her. The letters that passed between Catherine Booth and Queen Victoria are among the most remarkable documents in the literature of correspondence. Mr. Gladstone attached the greatest weight to her judgement and convictions. Bishop Lightfoot, one of the most distinguished scholars of his time, has testified to the powerful influence which she exerted over him. And, while the loftiest among men honored her, the lowliest loved her.

Such strong lives have their secrets. Mrs. Booth had hers. Her secret was *a text*. As a child she learned it by heart; as a girl she pinned her faith to the promise it enshrined; amid the stress and strain of a stormy and eventful life she trusted it implicitly; and, with all the tenacity of her keen, clear intellect, she clung to it at the last. In the standard *Life of Catherine Booth*—a huge work of a thousand pages—four chapters are devoted to the scenes at the deathbed. And then we read: 'The lips moved as though desiring to speak. Unable, however, to do so, the dying woman pointed to a wall-text, which had for a long time been placed opposite to her, so that her eyes could rest upon it.

MY GRACE
IS
SUFFICIENT FOR THEE

It was taken down and placed near her on the bed. But it was no longer needed. The promise had been completely fulfilled.'

'That,' said a speaker at one of the great Memorial Meetings in London, some of which were attended by many thousand people, 'that was her text!' And, as so often happens, her text explains her character.

For, considered apart from the text, the character is an insoluble enigma. It is like a consequence without a cause. I was talking a week or two ago with an old man, who, in

Australia's earlier days, did a good deal of pioneering in the heart of the bush.

'Once,' he told me, 'soon after I first came out, I really thought that I had reached the end of everything. I was hopelessly lost. My strength was utterly exhausted. I had gone as far as I could go. The country around me was flat and dry; my thirst was a perfect agony; and my poor dog followed at my heels, her tongue hanging out, and her sides panting pitifully. We had not seen water for several days. I sat down under a great gum-tree, hoping that an hour's rest would bring me fresh heart and new vigor. I must have fallen asleep. When I awoke, Fan was standing near me, wagging her tail. She seemed contented and satisfied; her tongue no longer protruded. An hour or two later, I suddenly missed her; she had vanished in the scrub. She was away about twenty minutes. I determined to watch her. Presently she set out again, and I followed. Surely enough, she had found a tiny spring in a slight hollow about half a mile away; and by that spring we were saved.'

I have seen something like this in a higher realm. I recall, for example, Richard Cecil's story of his conversion. Richard Cecil—the friend and biographer of John Newton—was one of the great evangelical forces of the *eighteenth* century, as Catherine Booth was of the *nineteenth*. But, in his early days, Richard Cecil was a sceptic. He called himself an infidel, but he was honest in his infidelity. He could face facts, and the man who can look facts fairly in the face is not far from the kingdom of God. Richard Cecil was not, his scepticism notwithstanding. 'I see,' he says, in telling us of the line of thought that he pursued as he lay in bed one night, 'I see two unquestionable facts.' And what were they? They both concerned his mother.

'*First,* my mother is greatly afflicted in circumstances, body and mind; and I see that she cheerfully bears up under all her suffering by the support that she derives from constantly retiring to her quiet room and her Bible.

'*Second,* my mother has a secret spring of comfort of which I know nothing; while I, who give an unbounded loose to my appetites, and seek pleasure by every means, seldom or never find it. If, however, there is any such secret in religion, why may I not attain to it as well as my mother? I will immediately seek it!'

He did; and those who are familiar with his life-story know of the triumphant result of that quest. It was precisely so with Mrs. Booth. Her children knew that, like the bushman's collie, she found refreshment at some secret spring. Later on, she told them of the text and led them, one by one, to the fountains of grace. '*My grace is sufficient for thee.*' And when, at last, the avenues of speech and hearing were closed, they hung the golden words before her clouding eyes. Again she greeted them with rapture, and, with unwavering confidence, pointed her children to their deathless message.

II

In his *Grace Abounding,* John Bunyan tells us that there was a period in his spiritual history when his soul was like a pair of scales. It partook of three phases. At one time the right-hand balance was down and the left-hand empty and high; then for awhile they were exactly and evenly poised;

and, at the last, the left-hand balance dropped and that on the right-hand was swinging in the air.

At the *first* of these stages he was being tormented about the unpardonable sin. He reminded himself that, for Esau, there was no place for repentance; and he felt that there was none for him. The scale in which he laid his despair was heavily weighted; the scale in which he placed his hope was empty!

And the *second* stage—the stage that leveled the balances? 'One morning,' he says, 'as I was at prayer, and trembling with fear, lest there should be no word of God to help me, that piece of a sentence darted in upon me: *My grace is sufficient!* At this I felt some stay as if there might yet be hope. About a fortnight before, I had been looking at this very scripture, but I then thought that it could bring me no comfort, and I threw down the book in a pet. I thought that the grace was not large enough for me! No, not large enough! But now it was as if the arms of grace were so wide that they could enclose not only me but many more besides. And so *this* about the sufficiency of grace and *that* about Esau finding no place for repentance would be like a pair of scales within my mind. Sometimes one end would be uppermost and sometimes again the other; according to which would be my peace or trouble.'

And the *third* stage—the triumphant stage? Bunyan felt that the scales were merely level because, in the balance that contained the hope, he had thrown only four of the six words that make up the text. '*My grace is sufficient*'; he had no doubt about that, and it gave him encouragement. But '*for thee*'; he felt that, if only he could add those words to the others, it would turn the scales completely. 'I had hope,' he says, 'yet because the *"for thee"* was left out, I was not contented, but prayed to God for *that* also. Wherefore, one day, when I was in a meeting of God's people, full of sadness and terror, these words did with great power suddenly break in upon me; *My grace is sufficient for thee, My grace is sufficient for thee, My grace is sufficient for thee,* three times together. And oh! I thought that every word was a mighty word unto me; as *My* and *grace,* and *sufficient,* and *for thee;* they were then, and sometimes are still, far bigger than all others. Then, at last, that about Esau finding no place for repentance began to wax weak and withdraw and vanish, and this about the sufficiency of grace prevailed with peace and joy.' And so the issue was reversed; the scale that held the hope overweighed completely the scale that held the despair.

If it were not that others have passed through an identically similar experience, we should feel inclined to marvel at Bunyan's reluctance to cast into the balances the tail of the text: *My grace is sufficient—for thee!* It seems strange, I say, that Bunyan should have grasped with such confidence the four words and then boggled at the other two. And yet it is always easier to believe that there is a Savior for the world than to believe that there is a Savior *for me.* It is easy to believe that

> There is grace enough for thousands
> Of new worlds as great as this;
> There is room for fresh creations
> In that upper home of bliss;

but it is much harder to believe that there is grace and room *for one.* Martin Luther believed implicitly and preached confidently that Christ died for all mankind, long before he could persuade himself that Christ died for Martin Luther. John Wesley crossed the Atlantic that he might proclaim the forgiveness of sins to the Indians; but it was not until he was verging upon middle life that he realized the possibility of the forgiveness of his own.

It is all very illogical, of course, and very absurd. If we can accept the *four* words, why not accept all six? If we credit the head of the text, why cavil at the tail? Sometimes the absurdity of such irrational behavior will break upon a man and set him laughing at his own stupidity. Mr. Spurgeon had some such experience. 'Gentlemen,' he said, one Friday afternoon, in an address to his students, 'Gentlemen, there are many passages of Scripture which you will never understand until some trying or singular experience shall interpret them to you. The other evening I was riding home after a heavy day's work; I was very wearied and sore depressed; and, swiftly and suddenly as a lightning flash, that text laid hold on me: *My grace is sufficient for thee!* On reaching home, I looked it up in the original, and at last it came to me in this way. MY *grace is sufficient for* THEE! "Why," I said to myself, "I should think it is!" and I burst out laughing. I never fully understood what the holy laughter of Abraham was like until then. It seemed to make unbelief so absurd. It was as though some little fish, being very thirsty, was troubled about drinking the river dry; and Father Thames said: "Drink away, little fish, my stream is sufficient for thee!" Or as if a little mouse in the granaries of Egypt, after seven years of plenty, feared lest it should die of famine, and Joseph said: "Cheer up, little mouse, my granaries are sufficient for thee!" Again I imagined a man away up yonder on the mountain saying to himself: "I fear I shall exhaust all the oxygen in the atmosphere." But the earth cries: "Breathe away, O man, and fill thy lungs; my atmosphere is sufficient for thee!" ' John Bunyan enjoyed a moment's merriment of the same kind when he threw the last two words into the scale and saw his despair dwindle into insignificance on the instant.

III

Some such thought shines through the passage in which Paul tells us how the great words came to him. He was irritated by his thorn; he prayed repeatedly for its removal; but the only answer that he received was this: *My grace is sufficient for thee!* Grace sufficient for a thorn! It is an almost ludicrous association of ideas!

It is so easy for Bunyan to believe that the divine grace is sufficient for the wide, wide world; it is so difficult to realize that it is sufficient for him!

It is so easy for Wesley to believe in the forgiveness of sins: it is so difficult for him to believe in the forgiveness of his own!

It is so easy for Paul to believe in the grace that is sufficient to redeem a fallen race: it is so difficult for him to believe in the grace that can fortify him to endure his thorn!

And yet, in a fine essay on *Great Principles and Small Duties,* Dr. James Martineau has shown that it is the lowliest who most need the loftiest; it is the tiny thorn that calls for the most tremendous grace. The gravest mistake ever made by educationalists is, he says, the mistake of supposing that those who know little are good enough to teach those who know less. It is a tragedy, he declares, when the master is only one stage ahead of his pupil. 'The ripest scholarship,' he maintains, 'is alone qualified to instruct the most complete ignorance.' Dr. Martineau goes on to show that a soul occupied with great ideas best performs trivial duties. And, coming to the supreme example of his subject, he points out that 'it was the peculiarity of the Savior's greatness, not that He stooped to the lowliest, but that, without stooping, He penetrated to the humblest wants. He not simply stepped aside to look at the most ignominious sorrows, but went directly to them, and lived wholly in them; scattered glorious miracles and sacred truths along the hidden by-paths and in the mean recesses of existence; serving the mendicant and the widow, blessing the child, healing the leprosy of body and of soul, and kneeling to wash even the traitor's feet.' Here is a strange and marvelous and beautiful law! The loftiest for the lowliest! The greatest grace for the tiniest thorn!

Is it any wonder that, this being so, Paul felt that his splinter positively shone? '*I will glory in it,*' he cried, '*that the power of Christ may be billetted upon me.*' He feels that his soul is like some rural hamlet into which a powerful regiment has marched. Every bed and barn is occupied by the soldiers. Who would not be irritated by a splinter, he asks, if the irritation leads to such an inrush of divine power and grace? It is like the pain of the oyster that is healed by a pearl.

And so, with Paul as with Bunyan, the grace turns the scales. It is better to have the pain if it brings the pearl. It is better to have a thorn in the one balance if it brings such grace into the opposite balance that one is better off. *With*

the thorn than *without* it. Therein lies life's deepest secret—
the secret that Catherine Booth and John Bunyan learned
from the lips that unfolded it to Paul. In *The Master's Vio-
lin,* Myrtle Reed tells us the secret of the music that the old
man's fingers wooed from the Cremona. 'You have but to
look at the master,' she says, 'and you will comprehend.'
There he stands, a stately figure, gray and rugged, yet with
a certain graciousness; simple, kindly, and yet austere; one
who had accepted his sorrow, and, by some alchemy of the
spirit, transmuted it into universal compassion, to speak,
through the Cremona, to all who could understand!'

That is the secret—the old musician's secret; Catherine
Booth's secret; Bunyan's secret; Paul's secret; the secret of all
who have learned the text *by heart!*

My grace is sufficient for thee—the inrush of the grace
turned Paul's torturing splinter into a cause for life-long
thankfulness!

My grace is sufficient for thee—the inrush of the grace
turned Mrs. Booth's fierce struggle into a ceaseless song!

My grace is sufficient for thee! To the man who, like
John Bunyan, stands weighing his gladnesses and sadnesses
with that text in his mind, it will seem that the one scale is
overflowing and the other empty. For it is the glory of the
grace that it takes what sadnesses there are and transmutes
them into songs sublime.

F. W. Boreham, "Catherine Booth's Text," *A Handful of
Stars* (London: The Epworth Press, 1922), 200-210.

WHITE ELEPHANTS

I cannot exactly claim the reverence and attention which
we all accord without stint or question to the hunter of
big game. I have never shaken the dust of civilization from
my feet and set off for the interior of Africa, the jungles of
Bengal, the Western prairies, or the hills of Ceylon. I have,
however, read all that Sir Samuel Baker, Major Stevenson-
Hamilton, Mr. Stewart White, and other big-game hunt-
ers have to say; and some of the most exciting moments I
have ever known have been spent in their very excellent
company. It is great sport to sit in a cozy chair in a sheltered corner of a shady verandah and to experience, one
by one, all the glorious thrills and indescribable sensations
of the chase. You hear the distant trumpeting of the herd;
you share all the hopes and fears of the hunter as he creeps
nearer and nearer to his quarry; you hear the great trees
bend and break as the angry monsters rush and charge; and
then, with a flush of excitement that almost makes your
heart stand still, you see the huge beast roll over beneath

the sportsman's magnificent aim. This is as near as I have ever got—or ever expect to get—to adventure of this heroic kind. Yet I have been doing a little big-game hunting on my own account. I have been on the track of white elephants; and certainly I have no reason to complain of lack of sport. None of the herds that I have ever seen described by visitors to Africa or Ceylon can compare with those upon which I have come in the course of my recent quest.

Let me, after the approved fashion of literary sportsmen, begin by describing the creature. And here the subject becomes instantly complicated, for there are, I must explain, several varieties of the beast. There are white elephants *and* white elephants. In its original setting the term connoted 'a gift which occasions the recipient more trouble than it is worth; a white elephant being a common gift of the Kings of Siam to a courtier they wished to ruin.' Nobody would suggest that, in this sinister form, the phenomenon is particularly conspicuous among us. At the opposite pole, it may be reasonably maintained that all the operations of the ordinary commercial world resolve themselves into a perfectly innocuous bartering and marketing of white elephants. Here is a grocer with tons of sugar in his cellar. What does he want with tons of sugar? Considered only in relation to himself, his stock is a white elephant; but he deliberately finds houseroom for that white elephant in order that he may serve his customers and enrich himself in the process. The same thought inevitably occurs to one on being shown the prodigious stores of any other tradesman. The miles of neatly folded materials on the shelves of the draper; the casks of drugs and powders in the storeroom of the chemist; the formidable array of carcasses displayed by

the enterprising butcher,—these represent so many remind-
ers of the fact that the commerce of life is largely manip-
ulated by the wholesale purchase of white elephants. But
between these two interpretations of the phrase—the one
as repugnant as the other is serviceable—there is another
phase of the matter; and it is this aspect of the question that
has brought me to my desk. It is this particular variety of
white elephant that I have just been hunting.

Surprising as it may seem, I came upon a very large
herd of white elephants almost under the shadow of Windsor Castle. A newspaper lying at this moment on my desk
tells of a White Elephant Exchange, inaugurated under
royal auspices and opened by Princess Alexander of Teck,
which was the other day conducted at Windsor. The white
elephants concerned consisted of various articles which the
donors found in their possession but for which they had no
real use. Each donor received as he entered the exchange a
ticket bearing a number, which entitled him to somebody
else's white elephant; and if he did not fancy the gift which
fell to his lot, he returned it, and it was sold for the aug-
mentation of the patriotic funds. It is averred that when
those who desired to assist in this original form of philan-
thropy ransacked their homes in search of white elephants,
they were astonished at the multiplicity and variety of those
animals to be found among their household goods. I can
easily believe it. Some time ago the residents of the city in
which I dwell were invited to search their homes in a very
similar quest, and to donate to patriotic purposes any goods
or chattels for which they had no further use. Carts passed
along the streets to convey these articles to the auction
rooms. You never saw such a procession of white elephants!

No menagerie since the world began could hold a candle to it. Comedy and tragedy jostled each other in the roadway. Here were the toys of little children who had passed beyond the need of all such entertainment; here was an old-fashioned mangle and a still older spinning-jenny; and here were ramshackle old bits of furniture that had long ago given place to successors of a later pattern, and had since their displacement, only littered up the house.

As I passed, in the course of my hunt, from one herd of white elephants to another, I was driven to the conclusion that our haphazard and somewhat ridiculous etiquette of gift-giving has something to do with the enormous quantities of game that I discovered. There are certain occasions—weddings, birthdays, Christmas, and the like—when, according to our present social usage, decency demands that a present shall be sent. Nobody would rebel very bitterly against this engaging custom if only his mind could be entirely emancipated from the torturing apprehension that, sooner or later, the dainty gift which he is at such pains to purchase will take its place among the melancholy ranks of the white elephants. Nine times out of ten the unwritten law that renders a present mandatory forbids any sane investigation as to the desires or requirements of the prospective recipient. It is equally indelicate, if not actually impossible, to ascertain the intentions of other donors. The result is inevitable. One has to determine between the dreamily aesthetic or the severely utilitarian. He purchases, in the one case, a beautifully bound *édition-de-luxe,* knowing that it will be rapturously admired and eternally unread; or, in the other, he fixes his choice on some eminently useful article, feeling as he does so that in all human probability half a dozen other articles almost exactly like it will be simultaneously received. And, in either instance, the danger of adding to the stock of white elephants is sufficiently grave to awaken embarrassing anticipations.

We ministers are sinners above all men on the face of the earth in this respect. We allow white elephants to multiply about us like rabbits in a district to which a gun never comes. Unless we take care, we shall be trampled to death by them. Look at our libraries—at least, look at mine! All round the room, into which I should be ashamed to show a lady, there are uncomely stacks of books that ought to find hospitality on the shelves. But the walls are crowded with shelves, and the shelves are packed with books. At least, it looks like it. But it is purely an optical illusion, and deceives everybody but myself. As a matter of fact, however, these latest arrivals, packed up so unceremoniously on the floor, are being cheated out of their rightful places on the shelves by an enormous herd of white elephants. There are books that we bought by mistake; books that we know to be valueless; books whose room is of much more value than their company. Yet, by an odd trick that books play upon us, we let them stay on the shelves while their superiors sprawl in undignified debasement on the floor! 'I have read,' says Sir W. Robertson Nicoll, 'I have read, and I find it to be true, that a man who loves books, unless he is exceptionally rich, is always more and more tormented to find room for them. They grow and grow, and the wall space does not grow, and the shelves do not grow. There is only one course possible, and it cannot be postponed for very long. The library must be weeded, and the weeding must be of a ruthless character.' This has driven me to make for myself a good resolution. I happen to have a birthday once a year. I intend for the rest of my life, whenever that auspicious date comes round, to set off after breakfast hunting white elephants. I shall go to the study first of all, and anybody who listens at the door will hear the thud, thud, thud, as the beasts fall upon the floor, and he will know that I am having good sport. And for a few days thereafter it will be reasonably safe for a lady to enter the room.

The problem is, however, capable of still larger implications. Looking round us here in Australia, it is impossible to blink the fact that the greatest problem in the development of the Commonwealth faces us just at this point. It is all very well for me to be sitting here beneath the Southern Cross calmly discussing the subject of white elephants. But what about Australia itself? Australia is a huge continent, only the southern fringe of which is at present being exploited. The remainder is to all intents and purposes a white elephant. How is it to be delivered from that obnoxious classification? The man who can satisfactorily answer that question is the statesman for whom the Empire is anxiously waiting.

And just once more. My friend Arthur Jenkinson is a good fellow. He is exceedingly popular in the office; he is always welcome at the club and in other places where men do mostly congregate. His wife thinks there is nobody like him, and his children clap their hands as they hear him come whistling up the gravel path. But that is as far as it goes. You never see him at church; he is doing no work for which the world will bless him when he is gone; and, as far as one can judge, he is laying up for himself no treasure in the world invisible. Years ago he sat spellbound at his mother's knee while she unfolded to him that sweet and gracious story with which no other story can compare; and in those days his unspoiled heart responded to its charm. The treasure of the ages was poured into his soul, but he has never made use of it. He has allowed the holy faith of his childhood to take its place among the ranks of the white elephants. It is like the family Bible on the whatnot—very precious, but never used.

F. W. Boreham, "White Elephants," *The Other Side of the Hill* (London: Charles H. Kelly, 1917), 198-205.

OUR RUBBISH-HEAPS

The great bush solitudes had taken the place of the bustling streets. He—an Australian minister on holiday—rested on a fallen tree beside the dusty track. He raised his hat to the loveliness and bathed his brow in the loneliness that pervaded everything. It was with him as when a great steamer stops in mid-ocean to allow her engines to cool. The thud of the propeller, the vibration of the machinery, are felt no longer; the stillness is uncanny. He drew from his breast-pocket his Bible, and, his mind recurring to his own attempts to build the city of God among the haunts of people, he turned to the stately old story of Nehemiah. He read on, undisturbed by the drowsy hum of insects and the merrier song of birds, until arrested by Sanballat's question: 'What do these feeble Jews? Will they *revive* the stones out of the heaps of the *rubbish* which are burned?' It was an awakening phrase—a *revival from a rubbish-heap!* He laid the open Bible on the mossy log beside him and lost himself in contemplation.

And, even as he pondered, a new object presented itself to his hungry mind. From the depths of the bush on the distant hill-side great wreathing columns of smoke curled skywards, occasionally shot through by fierce flashes of flame. Straining his ears to listen, he caught the crash of falling trees, and thought he could detect the crackle and roar of the fires as the monsters yielded themselves to the devouring element. Straining his eyes to see, he dimly discerned the figures of men moving here and there, super-intending the work of demolition and destruction. They were clearing away the maple and the myrtle, the wattle and the gum, to make room for the apple and the apri-cot, the peach-tree and the pear. And the preacher, as he watched, caught himself echoing Sanballat's question: 'Will they bring a revival out of a rubbish-heap? Will they obtain riches from refuse?' These were companion pictures—this picture in the Bible and this picture in the bush; and, as he gazed upon them side by side, several clear-cut thoughts emerged. He saw that rubbish-heaps fill a large place in the domestic economy of a world like this. And he saw that an element of such enormous magnitude must be governed by laws. Refuse must have its fixed rules. The slag-heap must have its statutes.

They have!

There is the law of *deterioration*. From the picture in the Bible and the picture in the bush it becomes clear that all material things, though as sacred as the Temple or as natural as the forest flowers, are on their way to the rubbish-heap. It sounds like a death-knell to the materialist. Materialism, unmasked, appears as the religion of the rubbish-heap. It is heavy tidings, too, for the ritualist; for Ritualism stands in

perilous relationship to the rubbish-heap. 'Now abideth'—
what? Altars? vestments? crosses? creeds? catechisms?
confessions? 'Now abideth faith, hope, love—these three;
and the greatest of these is love.' The moth is in our fairest
fabrics, and our holiest temples totter to their fall. 'And as
some spoke of the Temple, how it was adorned with goodly
stones and gifts, Jesus said: As for these things which ye
behold, the days will come in the which there shall not be
left one stone upon another that shall not be cast down.'
That is significant. It is well to set our affections on the
things for which the rubbish-heap can have no terrors.

There is the law of *occupation*. For Nehemiah, in the
one picture, and the settler in the other, find the ground not
fallow, but occupied. Moss and lichen cover every stone.
Giant trees, twining creepers, shapely ferns, and waving
grasses fight for every inch of soil. Rank weeds and spear-
like leaves peer out from all the interstices. Every crack
and cranny, every corner and crevice, is occupied. Nature
abhors a vacuum. Wherever the foot of man has failed to
tread, wherever the hand of man has failed to labor, God's
innumerable and invisible agriculturists plough and harrow,
sow and reap, and produce the bewildering beauties of
the bush. Hannibal's military precept of preoccupation
dominates the rubbish-heap. The moss and the lichen are
on the stones of Jerusalem because no Nehemiah has come
to build the city. The wattle and the gum abound on the hill-
side simply because no man has planted apricots or pears.
Is it not ever so? The mind becomes a wilderness of foul
imaginations because clean and wholesome thoughts have
not been planted there. The heart becomes, like Jerusalem,
a wilderness and a desolation because the kingdom of

Christ has never been established there. Evil evolves where good evacuates.

There is the law of *elevation*. The question is: What makes rubbish rubbish? The term is obviously not absolute, but relative. A lady's hat is a milliner's dream today. Tomorrow—a new style having come in—it is its mistress's despair. What has so suddenly changed delight to disgust, and made the fashion of yesterday the folly of today? It is the new style. And it is always the new style, whether of dresses or of Dreadnoughts, that flings the satisfaction of one day to the slag-heap of the next. What has made the maple and the laurel look like rubbish to the settler? The parrots and the kangaroos see no change to account for his vandalism. The aboriginals did not find it necessary to hack down trees and fire the undergrowth. Why, then, this fury of axe and torch and gunpowder? It is the conception of an orchard that has done it. That is the 'new style.' A man dreams of apples, and he burns the virgin bush. Then, in his orchard he sees the glint of gold! The soil is auriferous! The fruit-trees become firewood that he may seize the precious metal. Later on, in peril of a watery grave, he flings his very gold into the ocean that he may save his life. Bush, fruit, gold, each in their turn become rubbish, flung to the slag-heap by the alluring force of a higher attraction. Nor is life itself the last stage. The martyrs cheerfully threw even life away, fascinated by still greater wealth. Had not Paul his rubbish-heap? He counted all things but loss for the excellency of the knowledge of Christ Jesus his Lord, for whom he had suffered the loss of all things, and did count them but dung, that he might win Christ. The rubbish-heap can have no grander word written of it than that.

There is the law of *transformation*. God makes His loveliest roses out of rubbish. The charred ashes of yesterday's bush nourish the roots of tomorrow's orchard. If the refuse of the ages had been allowed to accumulate, the world would be uninhabitable. The air would be heavy with pestilence. We bury our rubbish, and it all comes back to us in fruits and flowers. Its resurrection body is divine.

It is just here that the Church finds her most acute problem. In every community there are crowds of people who have gone to the wall. They feel crushed and beaten. Under our fierce competitive system the iron law of the survival of the fittest has flung them on the social slag-heap, and they know it. They hate the churches, because the churches are old, and they think that if the churches had done their duty, things would not be as they are. They forget that, if the churches had *not* done their duty, things would be ten thousand times worse than they are. They snatch at every social quackery and political panacea. Now, the Church's mission is to do for this ruined mass what Nehemiah did for the rubbish-heaps of Jerusalem—to build out of them the city of God. 'Will they bring a revival out of a rubbish-heap?' asks Sanballat. Of course. A rubbish-heap is God's raw material. A revival is His finished product. Let the Church get to work. She alone is equipped for so divine a duty. If she fail, her collapse will be the disaster of the ages. In that melancholy event, this social rubbish-heap will become, like all untransformed rubbish-heaps, the menace of mankind and the peril of the world. In it all pestilential fever-germs will breed and multiply. Anarchisms and revolutions will fill the air with shrieks and screams. But the Church of Jesus Christ knows how to transform this mass of refuse into a field of roses. Paul understood the magic secret. He looked upon the unbridled lust, the grinding tyranny, and the hideous idolatry of the city of the Caesars, and was unabashed. And he gave his reason. The gospel, he said, is the power of God unto transformation. He saw that the foulest filth of Rome might become the fairest fragrance of the New Jerusalem.

F. W. Boreham, "Our Rubbish-heaps," *The Luggage of Life* (London: Charles H. Kelly, 1912), 147-153.

THE LUGGAGE
OF LIFE

Life is largely a matter of luggage. So soon as a child can toddle he displays an insatiable passion for carrying things. He is never so happy as when he is loaded. His face beams with delight when his back is burdened to the point of breaking. A few months later he cries for a wooden horse and cart, that he may further gratify his inordinate longing for luggage. And, if these appetites be not humored, he will exhaust his unconsecrated energies in pushing the chairs, tugging at tables, and carrying the cat. The instinct is there. You can no more deny him his load than you can deny him his lunch. The craving for both is born in him.

In his autobiography, Thomas Guthrie tells how the blood of the Scottish lads in his native village was stirred as the echoes of Waterloo reached that remote hamlet. 'Many a time,' he says, 'did we boys tramp a mile or two out of town to meet troops marching to the war, and proud we were to be allowed to carry a soldier's musket, which the poor fellows, burdened with all the heavy accoutrements of those days, and wearied with a twelve-hour march on a hot summer's day, were glad enough to resign to us.' Here is the same subtle law in operation. Man often loves without knowing that he loves; and, little as he suspects it, he is deeply in love with his load. He groans beneath it, as a man grumbles at the wife of his bosom, but, if it were taken from him, he would be almost as disconsolate as if *she* were taken from him.

When we were boys at school we learned ludicrous lessons about the weight of the air. How we laughed as we listened to the doctrines of Torricelli, and heard that every square inch of surface has to sustain a weight of fifteen pounds! How we roared in our rollicking skepticism when our schoolmasters assured us that we were each of us being subjected to a fearful atmospheric pressure of no less than fourteen tons! But Mr. H. G. Wells has drawn for us a picture of men unladen. His heroes—Mr. Cavor and Mr. Bedford—have found their way to the moon. The fourteen tons of air are no longer on their shoulders. The atmospheric pressure is removed; they have lost their load, and they nearly lose their lives in consequence. They cannot control themselves. They can scarcely keep their feet on the soil. The slightest spring of the foot, and they bound like a ball into mid-air. If they attempt to leap over an obstructing boulder, they soar into space like larks, and land on a distant cliff or alight on an extinct volcano. Life becomes weird, ungovernable, terrible. They are lost without their load. Which things are symbolic.

It is part of the pathos of mortality that we only discover how dearly we love things after we have lost them. We behold with surprise our affections, like torn and bleeding tendrils, hanging desolate, lamenting mutely the commonplace object about which they had entwined themselves. So is it with the lading and luggage of life. We never wake up to the delicious luxury of being heavily burdened until our shoulders miss the load that galled them. If we grasped the deepest philosophy of life a little more clearly we might perhaps fall in love with our luggage. The baby instinct is perfectly true. Our load is as essential to us as our lunch. Very few people have been actually crushed in this old world of many burdens. And those who have were not the most miserable of people. It will not be at all astonishing if the naturalists of tomorrow assure us that the animal world knows no transport comparable to the fierce and delirious ecstasy of the worm beneath the heel. It would only be a natural, and perfectly logical, advance upon our knowledge of Livingstone's sensations beneath the paw of the lion. At any rate, it is clear that man owes as much to his luggage as a ship owes to her keel. It seems absurd to build her delicately, and then burden her dreadfully. But the sailor loves the heavy keel and the full freight. It is the light keel and the empty hold that have most reason to dread the storm. Blessed be ballast! is a beatitude of the forecastle.

Such is the law of life's luggage. But the New Testament gives us a still loftier and lovelier word: 'Bear ye one another's burdens, and so fulfil the law of Christ.' And these laws—the law of nature and the law of Christ—are not conflicting, but concordant. The one is the bud, the other is the blossom. For Christ came, not to remove life's luggage, but to multiply our burdens. It is true, of course, that He said: 'Come unto Me, all ye that labor and are heavy laden,' but He only invited them that He might offer them His yoke and His burden. Here is something worth thinking about. Christ gives rest to the heart by giving burdens to the shoulders. And, as a matter of fact, it is in being burdened that we usually find rest.

The Old Testament records the sage words of an old woman in addressing two younger ones: 'The Lord grant,' said Naomi, 'that ye may find rest, each of you, in the house of her husband!' Who ever heard of a woman finding rest *in the house of her husband?* And yet, and yet! The restless hearts are not the hearts of wives and of mothers, as many a lonely woman knows. There is no more crushing load than the load of a loveless life. It is a burden that is often beautifully and graciously borne, but its weight is a very real one. The mother may have a bent form, a furrowed brow, and worn, thin hands; but her heart found its rest for all that. Naomi was an old woman; she knew the world very well, and her words are worth weighing. Heavy luggage is Christ's strange cure for weary hearts.

The law of life's luggage—the 'law of Christ'—has a racial application. It is notorious that a Christian people is not physically more robust than a savage people. Readers of Alfred Russet Wallace's *Travels on the Amazon* will remember that, the farther the intrepid voyager proceeded up the great waterway, the finer became the physique of the natives. And at last, when Dr. Wallace reached a point to which no white man had ever before penetrated, he discovered men and women any of whom might have posed as models for Grecian sculptors. The reason is obvious. The savage knows nothing of 'the law of Christ.' He will bear no other's burden. The sick must die; the wounded must perish; the feeble must go to the wall. Only the mightiest and most muscular survive and produce another generation. 'The law of Christ' ends all that. The luggage of life must be distributed. The sick must be nursed; the wounded must be tended; the frail must be cherished. These, too, must be permitted to play their part in the shaping of human destiny. They also may love and wed, and become fathers and mothers. The weaknesses of each are taken back into the blood of the race. The frailty of each becomes part of the common heritage. And, in the last result, if our men are not all Apollos, and if our women do not all resemble Venus de Medici, it is largely because we have millions with us who, but for 'the law of Christ,' operating on rational ideals, would have had no existence at all. In a Christian land, under Christian laws, we bear each other's burdens, we carry each other's luggage. It is the law of Christ, the law of the cross, a sacrificial law. The difference between savagery and civilization is simply this, that we have learned, in our very flesh and blood, to bear each other's burdens and so fulfil the law of Christ.

We set out with Dr. Guthrie. Let us return to him. He is excellent company. He is describing, with a glow of satisfaction, one of the ragged-schools he established in Edinburgh. 'I remember,' he says, 'going down the High Street early one morning and seeing a number of our children coming up. One of them was borne on the shoulders of another, and, on my asking the reason, he said that the little fellow had burned his foot the night before, and he was carrying him to school. That,' said the doctor emphatically, 'would not have happened in any other school in Edinburgh.' It is a parable. It is the law of life's luggage. It is the law of Christ.

F. W. Boreham, "The Luggage of Life," *The Luggage of Life* (London: Charles H. Kelly, 1913), 3-9.

WAITING FOR THE TIDE

Sauntering through the Melbourne Art Gallery—a favorite haunt of mine—on Friday afternoon, I was captivated by a picture that I had never seen before. I need scarcely say, therefore, that it was not hanging on the wall. The people who visit the galleries are always worth watching. On Friday my wayward eyes were arrested by a young couple—she in brown and he in navy-blue—sitting in earnest conversation in front of one of the paintings. Whether they were a honeymoon couple or merely sweethearts, I cannot say: her left hand was provokingly gloved: but it does not matter, the question is of moment to nobody but themselves. She was leaning forward—face in hands, and elbows on knees—absorbed in the study of a picture. He was eyeing it less intently, yet with genuine interest, moved thereto partly by the skill of the artist and partly by the infection of her enthusiasm.

The picture was Mr. Arthur Boyd's *Waiting for the Tide*. It represents a sheltered and tranquil cove in which a couple of boats are lying. The boat in the foreground is occupied by two men. They are doing nothing, for there is nothing to be done. The boat leans heavily over, showing that it is hard and fast upon the muddy bed of the little inlet. Until the tide comes swelling in, lifting and liberating it, its occupants are helpless. But their presence in the boat sufficiently indicates their determination to ply their oars and leave the bay the moment that the waters rise. Till then they are waiting—idly waiting—eagerly waiting—watchfully waiting—waiting, just *waiting for the tide!*

'It reminds one,' I heard the young fellow in navy-blue remark, as I slowly passed behind them, 'it reminds one of Mr. Micawber waiting for something to turn up!'

I did not catch her reply: I should dearly like to have done so. I hope that, being the wise little woman that she looked, she gently reproved his lack of penetration and discernment. The observation was as shallow as the water in the picture. For between the men sitting in their stranded boat, waiting for the flowing of the tide, and Mr. Micawber pusillanimously waiting for something propitious to happen, there is all the difference in the world. Having had a good look at the picture, let us submit Mr. Micawber to a similar scrutiny.

It is in the eleventh chapter of *David Copperfield* that we are introduced to Mr. Micawber. He is, as ever, on the brink of ruin; and, as ever, he alternates with lightning rapidity, between the heights of ecstasy and the depths of despair. 'It was nothing unusual for him to begin a conversation by sobbing violently and to finish it by bursting into song. I have known him,' says David Copperfield, 'I have known him to come home to supper with a flood of tears and a declaration that nothing was now left but a gaol; and go to bed making a calculation of the expense of fitting the house with bow-windows, *in case anything turned up.* This,' David adds, 'was his favorite expression.'

Three pages further on, Mr. Micawber is contemplating his release from prison under the Insolvent Debtors' Act. 'And then,' he exclaims, 'I shall, please Heaven, begin to live in an entirely new manner if—if—if, in short, if *anything turns up!'*

I turn three more pages and find Mr. Micawber, out of the bitterness of his own experience, pouring sage counsel into the ears of David. 'My dear young friend,' he says, 'I am older than you; a man of some experience in life, and—and of some experience in difficulties, generally speaking. At present, and *until something turns up* (which I am, I may say, hourly expecting) I have nothing to bestow but advice.'

And so on. In the daytime Mr. Micawber mingles with the throng upon the city streets, hoping for *something to turn up* among the faces that he meets there. In the evening he throws himself into his chair, adjusts his spectacles, and settles down to the newspaper, 'just to see whether *anything turns* up among the advertisements.'

There, then, is Mr. Micawber! Anything more unlike the boatmen in Mr. Boyd's painting it would be very difficult to imagine. Something may or may not turn up to gratify the baseless optimism of Mr. Micawber: as a rule nothing of the kind eventuates, and Mr. Micawber is left lamenting. But the tide! The tide is bound to turn! And not only so but it is bound to turn at a certain time. My morning paper tells me that it will be high water today at

8:57 a.m. and 7:51 p.m. Mr. Micawber's newspaper—the paper in which he expected *something to turn up* among the advertisements—never once mentioned the hour at which that nebulous and mysterious happening would take place! The men in the picture, on the contrary, know the exact moment at which the waters may be expected to come surging in; and they have everything in readiness.

That, in their case, is the beauty of it! And *that,* in Mr. Micawber's case, is the wretchedness and the pathos of it. Yes, the pathos of it! I think of W. J. Wills, the young astronomer and explorer, the most gallant figure among all our Australian pathfinders. The Burke and Wills expedition—the expedition in which, although only twenty-six, he was second in command—was the first to cross the continent. Leaving Melbourne on August 20, 1860, they reached the northern coast early in the following year. But disaster overwhelmed them on the return journey. Their supply of provisions gave out, and they were left to perish miserably in the hot and barren desert. Gray was the first to die. Burke, feeling that his end was near, attempted to stagger to Cooper's Creek, knowing that there his body would be discovered and taken to Melbourne for burial. Unwilling to see his leader go to a solitary death, King—the junior member of the party—decided to accompany him. Leaving Wills alone, the two set out into the wilderness. They had not gone far when Burke fell upon the sands, and King hurried back to Wills. But, during the absence of his comrades, Wills, too, had passed away. And there, lying near the body, was his journal, kept as was Burke's, to the very last:

'*Here I am,*' says the final entry, '*here I am, waiting, like Mr. Micawber, for something to turn up!*'

There lay the pathos of it! Waiting, *like Mr. Micawber!* In that brave young heart of his, Wills knew that, as in Mr. Micawber's case, nothing was likely to turn up; but he made up his mind to keep smiling to the last. *Waiting like Mr. Micawber!* There is an infinity of difference between *that* and *Waiting for the Tide!*

The *something* for which Mr. Micawber and our gallant young explorer are waiting—is a spectral contingency, a remote possibility, a shadowy chance, a forlorn hope. The *tide*—for which these boatmen are waiting—is the natural representative of those stable and reliable forces that dominate life at every turn. The tide stands for the stately dependabilities by which we are encompassed and surrounded. The masterly mechanism of the universe—the rising and the setting of the sun; the persistence in their orbits of the stars; the paths of the planets; the phases of the moon; the revolution of the earth; the cycle of the seasons; the round of the year—all this, like the ebbing and the flowing of the tide, is wonderfully reliable. The astronomers tell us that a comet that was last seen shortly after midnight on March 3, 1603, will again make its appearance at 9:30 p.m. on September 17, 1962; and we know for certain that, on September 17, 1962, the dazzling phenomenon will again adorn the evening sky. The astronomers tell us that, in a few years' time, there will be a total eclipse of the moon, visible in such-and-such a latitude and at such-and-such an hour; and we know that, to the very minute, the earth will be darkened and the silver moon obscured.

Obviously, there is about all this nothing that savors of Mr. Micawber. We are not the children of chance. Life is controlled by a superb combination of certainties. They may, with the most implicit confidence, be waited for; and they will always prove themselves to be worth the waiting. The thoughtless observation of the young fellow in the navy-blue suit was hopelessly wide of the mark. I sincerely hope that his fair companion, with characteristic charm and sweetness and delicacy, demonstrated to him his egregious blunder and tactfully set him right. The tide represents our best friends—the friends in whom we can always trust: the friends who never fail—and since *she* is likely to be the truest, dearest, most constant friend that he will ever know, there is a sense in which the tide represents *her!* And it would be painful to think of him as leaving the Art Gallery without a clear perception of the essential difference between her fond fidelity and the phantom-like fickleness of the will-o'-the-wisp after which Mr. Micawber was perpetually dancing.

I find it singularly pleasant today to think of those young people—she in brown and he in navy-blue—sitting in front of Mr. Boyd's picture. I hope they remained there long after I myself left the gallery—long enough, at least, to become impressed by the subtle significance that lurks in the lovely canvas. If they did, they will make time, through all the happy years to come, for just such quiet and restful hours as they were enjoying together today. For the tide—the tide for which the men in the picture were waiting—is the emblem of all the leisurely things in life. The tide cannot be hurried; there is nothing for it but to do as the men in the picture are doing; you must *wait for it.*

We have accelerated the pace of almost everything. The wheels of life revolve a hundred times as swiftly as they used to do. We dash through the years at a break-neck pace.

And we have every reason to be proud of our achievements. But one cannot check a flush of pleasure at the thought that there are a few things—and those are the best things— that still jog along at the same old pace. An oak takes just as long to grow in my garden as it took in the Garden of Eden. The tide ebbs and flows today exactly as it ebbed and flowed in the days of the Pharaohs. It soothes the brain and steadies the nerves and sweetens the soul to fasten one's eyes for awhile on these leisurely and unhurriable things. They breathe a benediction of peace on all beholders.

If these young people—she in brown and he in navy-blue—are as wise as I suppose them, they will take the hint. In the years ahead of them they will be tempted to smile disdainfully upon the days when they loitered in Art Galleries and wasted time in doing nothing. To be forewarned is to forearmed; and therefore I forewarn them. Let them, as they sit in front of Mr. Boyd's, eloquent picture, pay good heed to the lesson that the tide is trying to teach them. The men in the boat may be in a perfect agony of impatience; it makes no difference; they must wait. The tide takes its time; it waits for no man: it compels all men to wait for it.

If these young people learn the lesson of the tide, I shall meet them again in the Gallery. It may be in ten years' time; it may be in twenty: I cannot tell. But, however pressing the claims of business and society may become, they will always contrive to set aside a few delicious hours in which they can sit at their ease, and sit together, luxuriating in the beauty of the world. If the hour appointed proves wet or cold or windy, they will come to the Gallery and enjoy the beauties of *Art*. If, on the other hand, the chosen day proves sunny, they will stroll in the fields, or ramble in the woods, or sit in the park and enjoy the beauties of *Nature*. The tide declines to be infected by the fever of the folk who wait for it; let the girl in brown and her lover in navy-blue take that hint.

Let no man misinterpret! The doctrine of the tide is not a doctrine of *Indolence:* it is a doctrine of *Activity.* In point of fact, the tide is never still. Although it does its work in a restful and leisurely way, *it does it.* And it does it well. It is ever so; the world's best work is done by those who never know the fret and fever of haste. In their impatience the boatmen may feel that the tide is slow; but they know that it is sure. And they know that, before so very long, the tide will bring them their priceless opportunity.

For the tide—the tide for which they are waiting—does not intend these men to spend their lives waiting with folded hands in the seclusion of a narrow bay. The tide, for which they have waited so impatiently, comes at last! And then, if they have the will for it, and the strength for it, they can leave the tiny inlet in which they have been enclosed, and court a more adventurous experience on the broad waters beyond the bay. And then, as they do business in deep waters, they will feel that the tide, which seemed so long in coming, was worth the ordeal of waiting, after all!

I wonder if those young people—she in brown and he in navy-blue—heard the picture whispering that secret to their hearts! The tide—so faithful and so sure—offers every man, sooner or later, the chance of escaping from the tiny cove of the *Here* to the broad bosom of the *Everywhere,* from the little bay of *Self,* to the infinite sea of *Service;* and they are life's most enviable voyagers who, when the sublime opportunity presents itself, are all alive and all alert, waiting, with oars in rollocks, to make the most of it. It is the hour of destiny. The kingdom of heaven pours its wealth into the heart of the man, who is ready when that hour strikes. He was waiting: but only *waiting for the tide!*

F. W. Boreham, "Waiting for the Tide," *The Nest of Spears* (London: The Epworth Press, 1927), 48-57.

THE CANDLE AND
THE BIRD

To all peoples there come, sooner or later, periods in which the maintenance of a Christian life and an evangelistic testimony becomes so extremely difficult as to seem almost impossible. This spiritual sterility may be precipitated by any one of an innumerable array of causes—the horrors of war, with all their attendant hatreds and excitements; a wave of materialism, frivolity, or sensuality; the concentration of the public mind on subsidiary issues; or some other development that tends to hurl serious thought into obscurity.

But, whatever the cause, such distressing conditions do emerge; and the thing to be remembered at those times is that this unhappy state of affairs represents, not the snuffing out of a candle, but the frightening away of a bird. The distinction is vital. If you extinguish a light, the act is final: you plunge the room into darkness without creating any illumination elsewhere. The flame does not flash into being in some other part of the house. But if you startle a bird, the gentle creature flies away and sings its lovely song upon some other bough.

Several illustrations of this essential principle confront us in the annals of the early Church. A time came when, at Antioch, the Jews refused Paul and Barnabas a hearing. 'Very well,' exclaimed the Apostles, 'it was necessary that the Word of God should first have been preached to you; but, seeing ye put it from you, lo, we turn to the Gentiles!' The light was not snuffed out. The bird flew to another bough, that was all!

A little later, the two Apostles journeyed through Asia, intending to preach the word in every city. But, to their dismay, every door was closed against them. They were amazed and bewildered. But when they reached the end of the long road and saw nothing but the sea in front of them, a vision was vouchsafed to Paul. He saw a man of Macedonia bidding him cross the intervening waters and invade Europe!

Think what these two transitions have meant to history—the evangelization of the Gentiles and the conquest of Europe! And when you have grasped their momentous significance, you will have realized the importance of the principle that we have set ourselves to establish. When the Church is overwhelmed by an apparently crushing reverse, it is never the snuffing out of a candle: it is always the frightening away of a bird.

I

That principle is inherent in the eternal scheme of things. On the ancient monuments of Egypt there are crude drawings representing the soul, in the form of a bird, leaving the body of the monarch or hero to whom the memorial has been raised. In the form of a bird, mark you! Even the ancients felt that death is not the snuffing out of a candle; it is the escape of a bird. There is a divine element in humankind—an element which no tomb can imprison. And, similarly, there is a divine element in the Church—an element that no persecuting fires can devour and that no convulsion can destroy.

It was a dark day for the faith when, in the seventh century, the Saracens swept through the world, obliterating the Cross, overthrowing the Churches, and converting into Mohammedan mosques the most imposing Christian and Jewish structures. It certainly looked as if a glorious light had been put out. Yet, at the very moment at which all this was taking place in the old world, something of infinite significance was happening on an obscure group of mist-enshrouded islands in the northern seas.

Paulinus and the other missionaries whom Augustine had led into England caught the ear of the court and of the people; the preparatory work of St. Columba in Scotland and of St. Patrick in Ireland began to bear fruit; and thus, while Christianity was suffering eclipse among the lands of Yesterday, it was laying a powerful and formative hand upon the lands of Tomorrow.

Similarly, on the very day on which the French mob tore the Cross from Notre Dame in Paris and angrily abjured the Christian faith, William Carey landed in India and claimed a new continent for the Savior whom France was renouncing. Both events took place on November 11, 1793. A pessimist in France would have regarded the act of the populace as the extinction of a great light: anybody who reviews the incident in the calm perspective of history can see that it was merely the frightening away of a bird.

II

I cherish the hope that, one of these days, a writer learned in such lore, and with a flair for such a task, will trace the influence of this principle upon the history of revivals. Few studies are more stimulating than the study of those tremendous movements that have swept like a divine fire across the various nations. They stir the blood and quicken to new life the most sluggish and apathetic soul. But the striking thing about these historic revivals is that they are so transient, so evanescent, so temporary. They never endure. And the fact that, although so obviously divine, they never endure, sufficiently proves that they were never meant to endure. Martin Luther used to say that a religious revival always exhausts itself in thirty years. Isaac Taylor set a more liberal limit: he fixed fifty years as the maximum period: no revival, he declared, ever lasted longer than that. But the question that immediately concerns us is not the question as to how long a revival can last, but as to what happens when it fades out. And the answer to that question is that it never fades out. If it seems to vanish at one place, it is only that it may appear at another. For the end of a revival is invariably the beginning of a revival. Its termination is never the snuffing out of a candle: it is always the frightening away of a bird.

Is there, in our own annals, or in the annals of any other country, the record of a revival comparable with the

Puritan revival of the seventeenth century? Beyond the shadow of a doubt, it was a period of divine illumination. Like the sunrise playing simultaneously upon many snow-capped peaks, the light was caught and reflected by many totally diverse but really majestic personalities. John Hampden, George Fox, and Samuel Rutherford, for example, have little or no connection with each other, yet each represents a focal point in this celestial movement. As we project our minds into that memorable time, the stately and satisfying figures, the sturdy and eloquent faces of Oliver Cromwell, John Milton, and John Bunyan, moving amidst a cloud of kindred spirits, leap at once to our minds. We instinctively feel that Puritanism was no frolic of circumstance, no freak of history. The movement that has left as its indestructible monuments such works as *Paradise Lost* and *The Pilgrim's Progress* can only be regarded as a heavenly revelation. The Puritans, as Macaulay says, were 'men who, instead of catching occasional glimpses of the Deity through an obscuring veil, aspired to gaze full on His intolerable brightness and to commune with Him face to face.' The entire country was made to feel that God was palpitatingly near: the hush of the eternal brooded over city and hamlet. With the light of heaven on their faces and the fear of God in their hearts, the Puritans overhauled and rearranged everything. They put the king in his right place, and the Parliament in its right place, and the Bible in its right place, and the Church in its right place; and they did all this by putting God in His right place; they enthroned Him as Head over all. It was a time in which earth seemed crammed with heaven, and the songs of the angels filled with divine melody the English sky.

It was very wonderful; but it did not last. The spirit of Puritanism decayed with the accession of Puritanism to political authority. As soon as it became fashionable to dress as the Puritans dressed, to talk as the Puritans talked, and to do as the Puritans did, all people became Puritans. They might have felt no regenerating power in their hearts, but they could at least wear drab clothing, allow their hair to fall about their shoulders, interlard their conversations with pious ejaculations and give to their children biblical names. And then, the movement having become rotten within, it quickly received its deathblow from without. Two years after the death of Cromwell, the Stuarts were restored to power. A swing of the pendulum immediately followed. The nation experienced one of those violent reactions that so frequently mark the pages of history. Paradise was lost.

III

No revival, according to Isaac Taylor, can live for half a century. Fifty years after Puritanism had achieved its crowning triumphs, England was knee-deep in mire. The glory had departed, and its departure had broken Milton's heart. Joseph Addison, who cherished the spirit and ideals of the Puritans in an age that had renounced and repudiated Puritanism deplored the fact that English standards and English manners had fallen to their lowest ebb. Politics had degenerated into an undignified squabble; society was as corrupt as it could very well be; music, art and literature were all degraded; the sports and pastimes of life were universally squalid and usually obscene; religion itself had become formal, sanctimonious and largely hypocritical. 'Even the saint,' says Addison, 'was of a sorrowful countenance and generally eaten up with spleen and melancholy.' And, worst of all, the number of people who saw anything to be deplored in all this was so small as to be almost negligible. Now the question is, did this degeneracy represent the snuffing out of a candle or the frightening away of a bird? Let us attempt to survey a wider horizon in the hope of sighting the tree to which the bird has flitted! And what is this?

On the morning of August 13, 1727—eight years after Addison's early death—a number of young people were gathered for prayer at Herrnhut in Germany. Count Zinzendorf, the leader of the little band, was only twenty-seven, and it is doubtful if any of the others were very much older. What happened they could never precisely define. All that they could say was that a radiant sense of the nearness of Christ suddenly visited them, and, when their little gathering broke up at noon, they 'scarcely knew whether they still belonged to the earth or had actually gone to heaven.' In telling the story of their lustrous experience to their friends, the wondering hearers quickly contracted the sacred contagion.

Thus was born the Moravian movement—one of the most intensely spiritual and most passionately missionary organizations of all time. Fifty years before William Carey had inaugurated the era of organized missions to the heathen, these inspired Moravians had undertaken the evangelization of the world. Within five years of that memorable meeting at Herrnhut, they had sent missionaries to the Negro of the West Indies and to the Eskimo in the frozen North, quickly following these experimental ventures by despatching evangelists, not only to every country in

Europe, but to the four quarters of the globe. See, sings
William Cowper,

> See Germany send forth
> Her sons to preach Christ in the farthest North;
> Fired with a zeal peculiar, they defy
> The rage and rigor of a Polar sky,
> And plant successfully sweet Sharon's rose
> On icy plains and in eternal snows.

When, later in the century, William Carey endeav-
ored to persuade the English Baptists to initiate a missionary crusade, he held in his hand the inspiring records of
the Moravians. Throwing the pamphlet on the table, he
exclaimed: 'See what these Moravians have done! Cannot
we follow their example and in obedience to our heavenly
Master go out into all the world and preach the gospel?'

Now the striking thing is that this impressive and
fruitful outbreak in Germany exactly synchronized with
the evaporation of the Puritan revival in England. It was
not that a light had been extinguished: it was that a bird
had been frightened away.

IV

But, like the English movement, the German movement
also spent itself. That never-to-be-forgotten meeting at
Herrnhut was held in 1727. While those young people were
passing through that Pentecostal experience, Voltaire was
bending over the finished manuscript of his first book. The
writings of Voltaire quickly captivated the mind of a young
German prince who was destined to be known to history

as Frederick the Great. Frederick at once entered upon an admiring correspondence with the brilliant Frenchman, eventually inviting him to share the splendors of his palace at Berlin. And, in the hurricane of materialism and militarism that swept over Germany under that regime, the Moravian movement shared the melancholy fate that had befallen Puritanism in England.

But had the light been extinguished? Was it that a candle had been put out or that a bird had been frightened? Mr. Spurgeon ushered in a new day by creating a popular atmosphere for evangelism. This was his supreme triumph. In his famous *Memoirs,* Greville graphically describes Mr. Spurgeon—whose physique struck him as singularly reminiscent of Macaulay's—preaching, at an ordinary service, to nine thousand people. It impressed him, as it impressed all thoughtful observers, as an arresting and epoch-making development. It forced the evangelical pulpit into the glare of public attention. The world was compelled to take notice. It made thinkable and possible the work of all those ministers and evangelists who have since captured the attention of the populace. And it is only when we attempt to estimate the spiritual, ethical, and civil value of the impact of Mr. Spurgeon's flaming intensity upon each individual unit in the surging crowds that flocked every Sunday with wistful hearts to hear him that we realize how generously and how vitally he contributed to the new order that sprang into being in his time.

And so we bring our study down to within living memory. Let no person become unduly depressed because, here or there, the good work seems to flag. If, with us, the sun seems to be setting, you may depend upon it that other people, far away, are gratefully greeting the dawn. In a public reading-room, I one day picked up a London journal in which I read a series of somewhat dismal letters concerning 'The Dearth of Conversions.' On the very same table I found a couple of magazines. One contained an article by Dr. A. W. Hitchcock, telling of the sensational progress of the work of God in Korea, while the other told of a single church on the Congo that is welcoming to its membership more than five hundred converts a year. And thus—

> ... while the tired waves, vainly breaking,
> Seem here no painful inch to gain,
> Far off, through creeks and inlets making,
> Comes silent, flooding in, the main.
> And not by eastern windows only,
> When daylight comes, comes in the light,
> In front, the sun climbs slow, how slowly,
> But westward, look, the land is bright!

So true is it that a period of spiritual sterility invariably represents, not the extinguishing of a candle, but the frightening away of a bird. I have here attempted but a few fugitive illustrations. It will be the duty of that happy historian who undertakes to expound the principle more exhaustively to show that there have been times when the holy flame has visited other lands than those which I have mentioned, flitting from Holland to Switzerland, and from hemisphere to hemisphere. Often it has confined itself to no national frontiers, but has swept across an area that has included many peoples. But the principle is the same. When we have occasion to lament the spiritual poverty immediately around us, we may be sure that the bird that has forsaken us is singing his lovely song, to somebody else's rapture, on a distant bough. And so it shall continue until that day dawns for which the Church has ever prayed, when the Holy Dove shall feel equally at home on every shore and the earth shall be filled with the knowledge of the glory of the Lord as the waters cover the sea.

F. W. Boreham, "The Candle and the Bird," *Boulevards of Paradise* (London: The Epworth Press, 1944), 103-113.

DOMINOES

'*What do you say to a game of dominoes?*'

I was never more surprised. He was the last man from whom I should have expected such a suggestion. But that is the best of living in this world. On the other planets things happen according to rote; you can see with half an eye what is coming next. But this world is a box of tricks, a packet of surprises. You never know one minute what the next minute holds in store. Everything is effervescent, full of snap and sparkle.

'*What do you say to a game of dominoes?*'

No sooner said than done. The little wooden box appeared from a cupboard in the corner. The black and white tablets were emptied with a clatter on to the table, turned face downwards, and divided between us. We arranged and examined them, and got to business. It is a very old game, and had a great vogue a couple of centuries ago. The sport consists, as everybody knows, in always matching your companion's piece. You must follow his suit, or you lose your turn. If he plays a six, you must lay a six beside it. If he plays a four, you must match it with a four. If you cannot respond to the challenge of his piece, you hold your hand and he plays again. But to miss your turn is to submit to a heavy handicap, for the player who first gets rid of all his dominoes wins the game.

And so we played at dominoes, following that first game with a second and a third. It occurred to me while we were playing that life itself is but a game of dominoes. Its highest art lies in matching your companion's pieces. Is he glad? It is a great thing to be able to rejoice with those who do rejoice. Is he sad? It is a great thing to be able to weep with those that weep. It means, of course, that if you answer the challenge every time, your pieces will soon be gone. But, as against that, it is worth remembering that victory lies not in accumulation, but in exhaustion. The player who is first left with empty hands wins everything.

I have already confessed that when my host made his abrupt suggestion last night, I was never more surprised in my life. He was the last man whom I should have suspected of a fondness for dominoes. If he had said billiards or bagatelle or draughts or chess, I should not have wondered in the least. But dominoes! I could scarcely imagine him playing dominoes! That is the pity of it. You never know how many people there are who are waiting for a chance of playing dominoes with you. The most unlikely people play at dominoes. Mr. O. Henry, in one of his short stories, tells of a remarkable interview between a burglar and his prey. The unhappy victim was in bed.

'Hold up both your hands!' commanded the burglar, pointing his revolver at the head on the pillows. The man in bed raised his right hand.

'Up with the other one!' ordered the burglar. 'You might be amphibious and shoot with your left! Hurry up!'

'Can't raise the other one,' pleaded the victim.

'What's the matter with it?'

'Rheumatism in the shoulder!'

The burglar stood for a moment or two in deepest contemplation.

'It's good for you,' he observed at length, 'that rheumatism and me happens to be old pals. I got it in my left arm, too!'

And then the pair proceeded to discuss the nature of their aches and pains; they debated symptoms, premonitions, and the effect of a change of the weather. Then they compared notes as to the respective merits of opodeldoc, witch-hazel, essence of evergreen, rattlesnake oil, Chiselum's Pills, Finkleham's Extract, Omberry's Ointment, Pott's Pain Pulverizer, Blickerstaff's Blood Builder, and a number of similar preparations. By the time they had exhausted the list they were the best of friends, and the burglar sympathetically helped his victim into his clothes.

You would never have suspected that the burglar was eager for a game of dominoes. But as soon as his victim explained that he suffered from rheumatism in the left shoulder, the burglar matched the experience with an identical one of his own, and from that moment the game proceeded merrily enough. The most unlikely people play at dominoes.

Or, if it be objected that Mr. Henry's story is merely a frolic of a vivacious and versatile imagination, let us turn from fiction to fact. From Mr. Henry's pleasant fantasies to the somber biography of a Lord Chief Justice is a far flight. I am very fond, however, of Barry O'Brien's great *Life of Lord Russell of Killowen*. And few things in the book are more striking than the biographer's story of the way in which his friendship with Lord Russell—then Mr. Charles Russell—began. 'In the summer of 1875,' Mr. O'Brien says, 'my father died, and, in the winter of the same year, poor MacMahon passed away. Within a few months I lost my two best friends in the world. It was a great blow and a great sorrow to me. One evening about six o'clock I went into the "Cock" to dine. I felt very miserable, and, I dare say, I looked it. I had just commenced my chop when in walked Charles Russell. I think there was not a man in London whom I liked less to see at that moment. I shrank from what I conceived to be his cold, hard, unsympathetic nature.' O'Brien tried to gulp his chop hurriedly in order to get away from his frigid acquaintance. But Russell came and sat at the same table right opposite him. 'He started the conversation. He spoke about MacMahon with a sympathy and a feeling which I did not in the least expect. Indeed, I never, I think, saw so complete a metamorphosis in any man as I saw in Russell that evening. It seemed to me that, while we talked, the whole character of his face changed. The hard, masterful look was gone. The disagreeable combative expression of the mouth had vanished. The eyes were soft and kind. The voice was subdued and low; and now and then a charming smile would play over his features, lighting up what was truly a noble countenance.' And thus began a friendship which lasted and deepened through many years. Now here was a surprise! It never occurred to O'Brien that

Charles Russell could respond to his friend's sorrow with a sorrow of his own. He never suspected him of sympathy. But O'Brien learned that day, as I learned last night, and as we all learn sooner or later, that the most unlikely people play at dominoes.

For the beauty of dominoes is that any one can play the game. You have but to grasp two essential principles. You must clearly understand in the first place that, at every turn, you must match your companion's play, laying a six beside his six, a three beside his three, and so on. And you must clearly understand in the second place that the whole secret of success lies, not in hoarding, but in spending. Victory lies in paying out the little ivory tablets with as prodigal a hand as possible. It is better in dominoes to give than to keep. It is better to play a domino with twelve black dots on it than a domino with only two. Dominoes teaches me to 'measure my life by loss instead of gain, not by the wine drunk, but by the wine poured out.' Anybody who can firmly grasp these two fundamental principles may become an expert and brilliant domino player.

One of the most accomplished players that I have ever met was introduced to me by Mrs. Florence Barclay. I refer, of course, to Mrs. O'Mara, the nurse, in *The Mistress of Shenstone*. Lady Inglesby had received news that her husband had been killed on active service at Targai, and she was being attended by Doctor Sir Deryck Brand. Turning suddenly to the nurse, Sir Deryck caught a strange look of dumb anguish in those quiet eyes.

'Mrs. O'Mara,' he said, with a hand upon her shoulder, 'you have sorrow of your own!'

She drew away in terror. 'Oh, hush!' she whispered. 'Don't ask! Don't unnerve me, sir! Help me to think of her only!' Then, more calmly, 'Only, only, sir, as you are so kind'—she drew from her pocket a crumpled telegram and handed it to the Doctor—'Mine came at the same time as hers!' she said simply.

The doctor unfolded the War Office message.

'*Regret to inform you that Sergeant O'Mara killed in assault on Targai yesterday.*'

'He was a good husband,' said the nurse, 'and we were very happy.'

The doctor held out his hand. 'I am proud to have met you, Mrs. O'Mara,' he said. 'This seems to me the bravest thing I have ever known a woman do!'

She smiled through her tears. 'Thank God, sir,' she said tremulously, 'but it is easier to bear my own sorrow when I have work to do for her.'

What does it mean? It means that Mrs. O'Mara had thoroughly mastered the two essential principles of dominoes. She had learned to lay her own experience of anguish beside the experience of Lady Inglesby; and she had learned that the secret of life lay, not in saving her heart's best treasure, but in spending it. She might have worried; but she worked.

She reminds me of Charles Lamb. Charles Lamb knew how to play dominoes. How, at every turn, he matched his sister's moods, laughing with her when she was in the humor to laugh, and weeping with her when she wept! It is a dramatic and tender story, the story of Lamb's compassionate ministry to his afflicted sister. Charles had himself known the horrors of insanity, and, after his recovery, he watched over poor Mary with a brooding and vigilant solicitude. He simply lived for her, and tended her until his death with a most affecting and beautiful constancy. 'Whenever,' says one who knew them well, 'whenever an approach of one of her fits of insanity was announced by some irritability or change of manner, Charles would take Mary under his arm and set out for the asylum. It was very affecting to encounter the young brother and sister walking together across the fields, bathed in tears, bent on this painful errand. They used to carry a strait-waistcoat between them.' Charles and Mary Lamb were playing dominoes, that was all. Against each experience of hers, he set a similar experience of his own. The charm of dominoes is that it always calls out your best. As I have said, it is better to lay down a tablet with twelve dots than a tablet with only two. The more I give, the richer I am. Lady Inglesby's grief appealed to all that was best in Mrs. O'Mara, and, matching heartbreak with heartbreak, she gave herself without stint. Mary Lamb's affliction appealed to all that was best in the gentle Elia, and, matching suffering with suffering, he gave himself without stint to his brotherly ministry. And both Mrs. O'Mara and Charles Lamb were brought nearer to success in life's great game through squandering the soul's treasure with such a lavish hand.

And what about Paul? Was not Paul a pastmaster at both the principles that govern a game of dominoes? He knew that the secret of success was not to save your pieces, but to get rid of them. 'Most gladly, therefore,' says he, 'will I spend and be spent for you.' And was there ever one as clever at matching his companion's play? 'I made myself a slave,' he says, 'that I might win the slaves; unto the Jews I became as a Jew, that I might gain the Jews; to them that are under the law, as under the law, that I might gain them that are under the law; I became as without law, that I might gain them that are without law. To the weak became I as weak, that I might gain the weak; I am made all things to all people, that I might by any means save some.' That was the greatest game of dominoes ever played!

And surely this is the secret of the wonderful appeal that the Cross makes to me. It is divine sorrow exactly matching human sorrow. 'Humanity,' as one of the greatest of our lawyers put it, 'has been deeply wounded somewhere.' So 'He was wounded for our transgressions; He was bruised for our iniquities.' He was crucified between two thieves as an emblem of the fact that He laid His anguish beside our human anguish, His heartache and heartbreak beside our own. In matching our sorrows He poured out His own divinest treasure without stint and without reserve. He gave everything; and, because He gave everything, He must win everything. Yes, He must win everything! The appeal of the Cross carries all before it.

The 'Lady of the Decoration' tells how, one Christmas-time, she gave a magic-lantern entertainment to the mothers of the Japanese children who attended the kindergarten. The little Japanese women, who had never seen a piano before, much less a magic-lantern, came in force. But they were unimpressed. 'I showed them a hundred slides. I explained until I was hoarse. I gesticulated and orated to no purpose. They remained silent and stolid. By-and-by there was a stir, heads were raised and necks craned. A sudden interest swept over the room. I followed their gaze, and saw on the sheet the picture of Christ toiling up the mountain under the burden of the cross. The story was new and strange to them, but the fact was as old as life itself. At last they had found something that touched their own lives and brought the quick tears of sympathy to their eyes.' They felt that here was One who had suffered just as they had suffered, One who felt exactly as they felt, One whose deep and terrible experience exactly answered to their own. He was the very Savior they needed; the match was perfect!

> How sweet the fitness betwixt Him and me!
> My sin needs grace like this, so rich and free;
> And weakness, helpless weakness, such as mine,
> Is needed to make perfect strength divine.

These Japanese mothers felt that the story that they heard that night fitted their lives as glove fits hand, as key fits lock, as domino fits domino. When the great wide world makes the same luminous discovery, then depend upon it, the conflict of the ages is over and the Christ has won!

F. W. Boreham, "Dominoes," *The Silver Shadow* (London: The Epworth Press, 1918), 11-21.

HE MADE AS THOUGH

As if He had no further interest in the fates and fortunes of his two companions, Jesus, on arrival at Emmaus, *made as though He would have gone further.* In the hour of their loneliness and loss, in the darkest moment of their bewilderment and mystification, He deliberately forsook them, leaving them to go their way while He went His. 'Everything comes to an end,' He seemed to say; 'the best of friends must part!' And, after all, they were merely a casual group of strangers who, meeting by chance on the road to Emmaus, had walked together from the city to the village discussing the politics and happenings of the day. Reaching one of their homes, the two disciples were about to enter when Jesus, the third member of the little party, bade them 'Goodnight' and *made as though He would have gone further.*

The illusion of divine indifference! It confronts us in the phenomena of Nature. What does the earthquake care about good people or bad people? It treats them all alike. So do the storm and the drought and the avalanche and

the flood. Nature, we say, is but another name for God;
yet such forces, even under God's control, show no consideration for character or piety. The same apparent indifference marks the movements of history. War, pestilence,
famine, fire—these things sweep across the world: they are,
we believe, divinely marshalled and divinely governed; yet
they overwhelm saint and sinner with equal ruthlessness.
The laws that govern our health and happiness are just as
inflexible. Disease and accident overtake the believer and
the unbeliever without the slightest differentiation. Infection and contagion are no respecters of persons. We tell
ourselves that all things are in God's good hands and that
all things work together for good; yet we seem to be in the
grip of titanic forces that are marked by nothing so clearly
as by their sheer indifference.

Jesus Himself behaved in the same strange way. The
disciples are at their wits' ends in the storm on the lake: He
calmly settles down to sleep in the bow of the boat. What
does He care? It was that sense of indifference that hurt.
Carest Thou not that we perish? Carest Thou not? A broken-
hearted woman entreats Him to have mercy on her afflicted
daughter. *But He answered her not a word!* Blind Bartimeus
calls to Him from the roadside: *Jesus, Thou Son of David,
have mercy on me!* But He takes not the slightest notice.
Whereupon Bartimeus calls out so much the more, and, as
in the case of the Syro-Phoenician woman and her daughter, Jesus yields to his importunity. And then there is the
case before us. The two disciples on the road to Emmaus
tell the Stranger of their terrible bereavement. Their Master
has been murdered! He walks by their side and discusses
the Scriptures with them in the most wonderful way until

they reach their destination. It is late. They are unutterably tired, for, after a particularly exhausting and depressing day, they have had the long eight-mile walk to Emmaus. As they throw open the door, He smiles, waves His hand and moves on. That is as far as His sympathy carries Him. *He made as though He would have gone further.*

I

Yet what else could He have done? The door that they were entering was the door of *their* home: not of *His.* He had no right to enter it uninvited. He did the natural thing: *He made as though He would have gone further.* If I put myself in His place, I see that He only did what, in the same circumstances, I should have done. Perhaps, in relation to all life's baffling problems and inscrutable mysteries, we should do exactly what God does if we could only put ourselves in His place.

It was the only thing that He could do, and He was secretly glad to do it. He was glad to do it because it was the only way of securing further fellowship with them. A young mother says 'Good-bye' to her tiny toddler on the floor, and moves towards the door. The little one begins to whimper at the thought of losing her; and she, having achieved her purpose, snatches him up and smothers his face with kisses. She merely wanted to be wanted. And so did Jesus; *He made as though He would have gone further.* And, filled with dismay at the thought of losing Him, they implored Him to enter and share their evening meal. *And He went in to tarry with them.* That speaks for itself.

It is clear from all this that we can have as much of Him as we will. If He leaves us, it is because we are quite willing that He should go. He may go; but, if He goes, He goes with our consent. On *His* side there is always the willingness to stay and stay and stay. Having loved His own which are in the world, He loves them unto the end. Ask Him to abide, and His divine heart instantly and eagerly responds. Those who are without His presence are those who do not desire His presence. We can always have Him if we will.

II

Life has its crucial moments. We come to the Emmaus door and He—*makes as though He will go further.* The idyll of the Emmaus road is repeated in the experience of every person. There is a sense in which, unrecognized, the Savior walks with each of us in the days of infancy and youth. We are conscious of certain impulses, aspirations, and yearnings: we know not from where they come. Conscience speaks; Reason speaks; Scripture speaks; the Church speaks; the Holy Spirit speaks; and, as a result of all these still small voices, certain impressions are made. But that state of things cannot continue indefinitely. Such voices are not mere music to be enjoyed: they represent mandates to be obeyed. In due course we arrive at the Emmaus door and realize that the moment has come to make a vital decision. *He makes as though He will go further;* and, unless we constrain Him, He certainly will.

The same thing often happens on a Sunday night. After a difficult and trying week in workroom, home or office,

Sunday comes. What a day it is! We revel in its gracious fellowship and joyous activities. The services; the singing; the
sermons; the people; the entire atmosphere of the sacred
day! It is Bunyan's Palace Beautiful all over again! And then,
suddenly, it comes to an end. After the walk and the talk
that made our hearts burn within us, we arrive abruptly at
the Emmaus door. Sunday is over! Our hearts miss a beat
and we catch our breath as we realize that only Monday lies
ahead of us. The beatific vision must vanish; the delicious
glow must depart: *He makes as though He will go further.*

III

Then came the thrill! The sensational moment arrived, not
on the road before the threatened parting, but at supper
after they had persuaded Him to remain. Perhaps by some
peculiarity in the way in which He gave thanks; perhaps
by some little mannerism in His eating and drinking; they
recognized Him! It was Jesus! They were not bereaved after
all! Their tears had all been wasted! Their desolating heartbreak had been needless! Jesus lived! He lived—and loved!
He was the same, yesterday, today and for ever!

And to think that this startling discovery had been
made, not in the heart-warming talk on the road, but afterwards, afterwards! It is often so. The vivid, palpitating sense
of His Presence comes, not on Sunday, but on Monday! We
feel, on Sunday night, that we are losing Him. *He makes as
though He is going further.* And, in our fear of such a calam-
ity, we do as these two men did at Emmaus. We implore
Him to remain with us. And He does. And, as in this case,
so in ours, the really sublime revelation follows.

It is Jesus! He is alive! They have nothing to sorrow about. They suddenly reflect that the others ought to know. John may be weeping his eyes out in Jerusalem; Peter may be tossing on his bed in an agony of grief; James may be pacing his lonely room disconsolate: they should be told! And so these two excited men set off the same hour of the night for the city. Late and all as it was; tired and all as they were; they took to the road afresh like a pair of excited striplings. And, with their hearts, not burning but singing, they hurried along those eight mortal miles that they might tell their brethren of the amazing revelation that had broken upon them at supper time.

Yes, life has its crucial moments. There comes a time when I have to make a momentous decision. It is not a question of going on in the same old way, or making a change. Those are not the alternatives. I have reached the Emmaus door. There is no question of going on: that is not the point. It is a question as to whether, on the one hand, I shall let the Savior go, or as to whether, on the other, I shall constrain Him to abide with me forever. If, standing beside that door, I let Him go, I miss the radiant revelation that, flinging a celestial luster over every commonplace day of my commonplace life, would have given me a mission that would, in its turn, have glorified the lives of others. But if, on that threshold, I invite my Lord to enter, I turn earth into heaven and transform every simple meal into a banquet of Paradise.

F. W. Boreham, "He Made as Though," *Cliffs of Opal* (London: The Epworth Press, 1948), 87-91.

THE WHISPER OF GOD

"Lo, these are the outskirts of His ways; and how small a whisper do we hear of Him! But the thunder of His power who can understand?" Job 26:14 (RV).

These words were written when the world was young. Yet they contain a scientific statement which the long file of centuries has not rendered obsolete: "Lo, these are but the outskirts of His ways." They voice a sentiment which expresses one of the most intense problems which are throbbing in the minds of thoughtful people today: "How small a whisper do we hear of Him!" And they contain a shout of triumph in which the saints of all ages may participate: "The thunder of His power who can understand?" We have here:

I. A TREMENDOUS TRUTH – "Lo, these are but the outskirts of His ways!"

    1. It obtains in the natural world.

I do not know how much you have seen of God's work. It may be that you have deeply and exhaustively explored it. You may have taken the telescope with Galileo, and Newton, and Kepler, and Herschel, and Ball, and scanned the heavens so thoroughly that the courses of the planets are your familiar paths, and the stars your most intimate friends. You may have descended into the earth with Logan, and Smith, and Dawson, and Carpenter, and Murchison, and Miller, until all the secrets of the rocks and the sands, the stones and the strata, have whispered themselves into your mind. With Ray, and Brown, and Bentham, and Lindley, and Hooker, you may have examined the ferns and the flowers, the mosses and the mammoth trees, until there is not a broken leaf or a crushed petal that does not unfold a revelation to your soul. The mysteries of all the arts and all the sciences may be mere commonplaces to you. But though you have all the -osophies and -ologies at your fingers' ends; though air, and earth, and sea, and sky have been unable to withhold any of their mysteries from you, yet of this I am certain—that you have but seen the shell and not the kernel, you have seen the part and not the whole. For, "Lo, these are but the outskirts of His ways."

And though, over and above this, you have followed the acts of God in the history of the ages; though you have sat side by side with Herodotus and Xenophon and Caesar, with Gibbon and Hume and Prescott, with Macaulay and Carlyle and F'roude; though you have done from event to event, from reign to reign and from battle to battle, saying to yourself: "This is the finger of God," yet have you only seen the outskirts of His ways. You must still stand like the great philosopher and say: "I am but as a little child, picking up shells on the shores of Eternity"; or, like a great English writer, you must confess: "I have but kissed the hem of the garments of God!" I am not surprised that the words that were considered most appropriate to be carved over the archway leading into our splendid museum at Christchurch were the words of our text.

The best of man's work is to be seen on the surface. He, to use an expressive colloquialism, puts all his best goods in the window. The more deeply you probe and search into his manufactures, the more you see of their imperfections, and the less you see of their beauty. Take a microscope to them, and the loveliest work of art is a daub; the finest production of the sculptor is but a rough-hewn block; the greatest masterpiece is full of flaws. Not so is it with the work of God.

The superficial observer admires the stars that bespangle the heavens at night—the "forget-me-nots of the angels," as Longfellow called them; but the superficial observer cannot admire them with one half the rapture with which the astronomer almost worships them.

A little child can admire a lily; but only the botanist can fully appreciate it. A landscape painter may be delighted with a piece of mountain scenery; but the geologist sees in it a greater grandeur still. With the work of man familiarity breeds contempt, and distance lends enchantment to the view. With the work of God the very opposite is the case. He who gazes upon the external loveliness of Nature may say: "How beautiful!" but it may always be added: "These are but the outskirts of His ways." And when Geology, and Botany, and Astronomy have laid bare a million million other beauties that you and I have never yet suspected, it may still be written in large letters on the title pages of all their works: "Lo, these are but the outskirts of His ways; how small a whisper do we hear of Him; but the thunder of His power, who can understand?"

Every discovery of Rontgen and Marconi and Edison, and of every other scientist, hints at the same thing. We never reach finality. There are always wonders on ahead of us. Every year, every week, every day, new marvels are unfolded and new secrets learned. And every such discovery leads us to write over all our wonderful appliances and comforts: "These are but the outskirts of His ways."

2. *What is true in the natural world is true also in the spiritual.*

(a) In Grace. Why, men and women, we often catch ourselves talking of the Cross of Christ, of the Atonement, and especially of "God's plan of salvation," as though it were a simple thing, and all its heights, and depths, and lengths, and breadths, fully and thoroughly and exhaustively explored by us. And yet, and yet! are we not led to suppose that that "plan of salvation" took an Eternity to arrange, that it has all the ages of Time as the theater of its operations, and that it will take another Eternity to reveal it? "In the ages to come He will show the exceeding riches of His grace in His kindness towards us through Christ Jesus." Eternity its birthplace; all time its arena;

Eternity its revelation. Why, the "plan of salvation" that *we* expound so glibly could have been invented by two ingenious minds in an hour, and revealed by them to any audience in another hour. And yet the Gospel of the Grace of God was the outcome of the eternal deliberations of the infinite wisdom of God. Take your pen, and then write of every sermon you ever heard, on every book you ever read, on all your "Bodies of Divinity" and systems of theology, and expositions of the "plan of salvation," and on every word concerning God you ever saw or heard, and for every thought concerning God you ever had, "Lo, these are but the outskirts of His ways; how small a whisper do we hear of Him!"

(b) In Glory. Think for a moment of the happiness which the very idea of Heaven has introduced into the world. Think of the poverty that has been made tolerable by it; the suffering that has been alleviated by it; the bereaved homes that have been comforted by it; the lives that have been ennobled by it; the deaths that have been irradiated by it. Then think how little we know of Heaven. Not even Scripture contains any description of it. "Eye hath not seen, nor ear heard, neither have entered into the heart of man

the things which God hath prepared for them that love Him." If so small a whisper of Heaven has brought such happiness into a weeping world, what will the full revelation be like? I do not say that all your ideas of Heaven are wrong; but I do say, fearlessly, that after you have read all your Poetry about Heaven; after you have pictured to yourself its streets of gold, its many mansions, its "sweet fields beyond the swelling flood" that "stand dressed in living green"; its angels and archangels, and all the gladness and the glory of it; after you have worked out all your imaginations and sung all your songs, you may still say: "Lo! these are but the outskirts of His ways; how small a whisper do we hear of Him!"

II. A TREMENDOUS MYSTERY – "How small a whisper do we hear of Him!"

Has it never occurred to you as an extraordinary thing that all Christendom is bowing down and worshipping a God Whom not one person has ever heard or ever seen? "How small a whisper do we hear of Him!" He rarely interposes in our affairs. Sometimes in earthquake, or tempest, or famine, or war, we get hints of His hand dealing with us, but only hints even then; a whisper, only a whisper, how small a whisper!

1. *This is the Mystery of Iniquity.*

Two young men enter business. One is unscrupulous, dishonest, scheming; the other is upright, straightforward, God-fearing. The first goes forward with a rush. True, it doesn't last long; but for a time it seems as though it pays best to be a rogue. The other is disheartened; he thinks it useless to be good. He murmurs and fancies God should intervene. "How small a whisper," he says, "do we hear of Him!" God is silent.

Two tradesmen set up in business. One is an angel; the other a devil. It is the devil who for a while sweeps the board. It is true that his path lies through fiery success to the bankruptcy court and the gaol; but men have not foresight; and for a while the angel murmurs against God for letting the wicked prosper and for saying nothing. He is angry that God is so silent. "How small a whisper do we hear of Him!"

Two farmers hold adjoining properties. The one is a Christian; the other an infidel. Harvest time comes. The grain is ripe; Sunday is a fine day. The infidel harvests his crop; the Christian worships God. Monday is wet; Tuesday is worse; Wednesday worse still. The Christian gets his crop in, damaged, on Thursday. He watches the sceptic get higher prices in the market. He wonders that the heavens over the infidel's farm are so beautifully blue. "How small a whisper do we hear of Him."

It was this that puzzled poor demented Barnaby Rudge. You know how Dickens tells the story. You remember how Gabriel Varden came upon Barnaby—the poor lunatic lad—at night, bending over the prostrate bleeding form of a man who had fallen a victim to highway robbery. "See," says Barnaby, "when I talk of eyes the stars come out! Whose eyes are they? If they are angels' eyes, why do they look down here and see good men hurt, and only wink and sparkle all the night?" "How small a whisper do we hear of Him!"

How skillfully Diabolus used this argument in Bunyan's famous allegory, when all looked black in Mansoul! "Oh, Mansoul," he cried, "consider that notwithstanding the old gentleman's rage and the rattle of his high and thundering words, *you hear nothing* of Shaddai Himself; you see that He values not the loss, nor rebellion of the town of Mansoul, nor will He trouble Himself with calling of His town to a reckoning for their giving of themselves to me!" "How small a whisper do we hear of Him!"

"It would be easy to believe in God," said Carlyle, "if He'd only do something; oh, that He would do something!" God is a silent God. "Oh, that Thou wouldst rend the heavens and come down?" sighed Isaiah of old, and many a person heaves the same sigh today. We are often tempted to cry, with the stricken Arthur:

> I found Him in the shining of the stars,
> I found Him in the flowering of the fields,
> But in His ways with men I found Him not.
> Oh, me! For why is all around us here
> As if some lesser god had made the world,
> But had not power to shape it as he would.

And yet, not altogether silent. A whisper; how small a whisper! But yet a whisper. A whisper in the heart of the honest young man in the warehouse; a whisper in the heart of the tradesman who watches enviously his evil rival; a whisper in the heart of the worshipping farmer. And that small whisper says it's all right.

God's in His heaven.
All's right with the world.

A whisper in the conscience of the rogue in the warehouse; a whisper in the soul of the unscrupulous shopman; a whisper in the heart of the Sabbath-breaking farmer. "How small a whisper!" but a whisper.

It says that right is right;
That it is not good to lie;
That love is better than spite;
And a neighbor than a spy.

It tells them that their prosperity won't last; it tells them that their iniquity won't pay. It tells them all this; in their heart of hearts they hear it; and, what is more, in their heart of hearts they believe it!

2.   *It is the Mystery of Godliness.*

There came a woman unto Jesus who prostrated herself before Him, and besought Him in agony and tears to help her. "And He answered her never a word." That is the mystery. It has baffled many. The awful silence of God. What does Tennyson say?

O mother, praying God will save
Thy sailor—while thy head is bow'd
His heavy-shotted hammock-shroud
Drops in his vast and wandering grave!

"How small a whisper do we hear of Him!" It was this that almost baffled some of the Scottish Covenanters, fighting and dying for truth and for conscience on the bleak moors of the far north. Robert Buchanan tells us, in describing the battle of Drumliemoor:

> How shrill and awful rose, 'mid the splashing blood and blows,
> Our scream unto the Lord that let us die;
> And the fiend amid us roared his defiance at the Lord,
> And his servants slew the strong man 'mid his cry;
> And the Lord kept still in heaven; and the only answer given
> Was the white snow falling, falling from the sky.

"How small a whisper do we hear of Him!" And yet, again, there is a whisper, though only a whisper. A whisper in the heart of the woman that tells her that silence is not callousness, and that Jesus will hear; a whisper in the soul of the praying mother that tells her that her prayer is heard, and shall only be denied her in order that she may have golden gifts instead of the silver trifles that she craves; a whisper in the hearts of the dying martyrs that assures them that all Heaven hears them, prospers their cause, and waits to welcome them Home!

For silence does not mean inactivity any more than noise means power. Hume tells us that, immediately before the Battle of Hastings, the English camps were filled with shouting and revelry while an awful silence brooded over the Normans. The silence that reigned along the British battle-line before Trafalgar has been the repeated subject of comment. And the most distinguished hero that European Protestantism ever claimed was known by the significant title of "William *the Silent*." The quietest room in a Lancashire cotton-mill is the engine-room. It is called the

"power room." A river steamer on the Thames is brought
to her moorings amid the wildest shoutings and the vilest
imprecations between the captain and the handful of men
that form his crew. A ten-thousand-ton liner is berthed at
Liverpool docks without the slightest shouting or confusion. Men make more noise in one hour's work in the harvest field than God's rain and sunshine and heat and cold
have made in producing the crops that they harvest. A man
makes more noise in clearing the snow off his front path
than the sun makes in melting a million tons of it. God is
so wonderfully silent because He is so wonderfully active.

For all practical purposes a whisper is enough. The
truth of a whisper is as great as the truth of a shout. A
whisper from God is enough to tell me that God is; it is
enough to tell me that He cares for me, for He whispers
to me. A whisper to the bad man, to the dishonest man,
to the unbelieving man is enough. Caesar was warned by a
whisper. He heeded it not, and went on to his death. But he
was as much and as truly warned as though all Rome had
thundered out "Beware!"

Moreover, I take this silence, this whisper, as a mark of
dignity. Singularly enough, the persons whom we reverence
the most are the persons who to us are silent. The greatest
men in the world are great silences to us. We have never
seen them; never heard them; how small a whisper do we
hear of them. And we reverence them because they are so
great as never to cross our paths. They would, perchance,
lose something of their dignified greatness if they came into
touch with us every day. It is the world's nobodies whose
voices we hear the most; it is the world's great ones whom
we rarely or never hear. One of our poets has said:

The Infinite always is silent,
Tis only the finite speaks.

"Speech," Dora Greenwell finely says, "is but a part of life's deep poverty." If God were to step in to miraculously prevent every injustice; to strike down every man who breaks His Sabbath; to paralyze every hand that steals; to silence every tongue that curses; what a little God He would soon seem to us! Instead of being august He would only be terrible; instead of being reverently feared He would only become the object of universal fright. The thunder is grand, awful, dignified, because it thunders so rarely; if it thundered every day it would become commonplace.

I sought for God in star-dumb space;
Beneath the seas I made a stair;
And laid the primal forges bare;

I asked if He were hid
'Neath cairn or pyramid;
I questioned rune and kann,
And bones as old as man.

There was no voice, nor beck nor trace,
To lull the ache of my despair;
My lattice-roses tapped my face,
And God was there!

"How small a whisper do we hear of Him!" Yet we do hear that small whisper; let us thank God with all our hearts for it, and with all our souls bow in admiration at the infinite silence of the Eternal. Consider,

III. A TREMENDOUS IMPOSSIBILITY – "The thunder of His power who can understand?"

The figure is, like all Scriptural figures, singularly appropriate. Thunder does not—especially in the East— come suddenly. There is the close, sultry, intolerable heat; the atmospheric disturbance; and then the final storm. God does not strike suddenly. He can afford to wait His time. He watches the Papal ships being built in every Spanish port; hears the clang of hundreds of thousands of hammers preparing the great fleet that is to sail forth to crush Protestant England. But He does not paralyze a single hand. Cannon are being cast in all the Italian ironyards, but no ironworker falls dead at his post. Soldiers are drilling and men being enlisted to take part in the Pope's final struggle for Britain. And no soldier is struck by lightning on parade. And England, fearful for the consequence of an attack by such a massive fleet, wonders that God allows it all. "How small a whisper do we hear of Him!" But wait! Thunder never comes suddenly. The huge fleet sets sail at last, and a hundred and forty-nine vessels threaten England off Lizard Point. And still God does not intervene. God might be dead for all England hears of Him; and ten thousand Englishwomen are on their knees calling upon Him amid their tears to save their dear old country from the Pope and the horrors of the Inquisition. The British fleet of eighty vessels under Lord Howard did their best for nine days; and still the heavens were cool, still women were praying, still men said: "How small a whisper do we hear of Him!" "Then came the suggestion, not of Drake, nor of Frobisher, nor of Hawkins, nor of Howard himself, but of a woman—the woman on the throne, Queen Elizabeth—the suggestion of the fire-ships, upon which Lord Howard acted; the plan that threw the huge Armada into hopeless confusion. But still there was no Divine intervention. And, if they could reform, England might be conquered yet. But the hour had come. The time was ripe. *God came.* A fearful gale arose upon the scattered, shattered fleet, and they were piteously driven northward before a remorseless wind. 'Mid thunder that rent the skies, and lightning that dazzled the eyes, many of the Spanish ships foundered at sea; many more were driven by the force of the gale on to inhospitable rocks. Over 8,000 men perished at one spot close to the Giants' Causeway, while on a single strand, near Sligo, an English captain counted eleven hundred Spanish corpses cast up by the waters. And then the men and women who had been saying for weeks: "How small a whisper do we hear of Him," finished the text, and exclaimed with thankful hearts: "But the thunder of His power who can understand?"

So must it always be. You who suffer and wonder that God does not intervene and rid you of your oppressions, be still, no matter how small the whisper that you hear of Him. "Vengeance is mine; I will repay," saith the Lord. His thunder shall burst out at exactly the right moment, and relief shall come. Like the garrison at Lucknow listening to the first distant sounds of the Highland bagpipes, you shall soon hear the hosts of God. However small the whisper that you hear of Him, you shall soon listen to the thunder that none can understand.

You who do well and suffer by it and you who do ill and gain by it! it is nothing that you hear but a small whisper of God as yet. The thunder of His power shall be unchained and shall break forth, utterly destroying the unjust, and gloriously justifying the righteous.

You who continue in sin and smile because no bolt strikes you from the blue, beware of His thunder! You have heard His whisper in your conscience. You may hear it no more. It is enough that you have been warned. Turn from your sin, I beseech you; turn to Him, and "He will have mercy upon you, and to our God, for He will abundantly pardon." But if you will not hear His whisper and turn, then, I tell you, in God's name, you must hear His thunder. Suddenly it shall burst upon thy frighted, trembling, guilty soul! The flash of His lightning shall lay thine whole life bare; and the words shall echo like thunder through thy soul, "Depart from me, ye cursed; the unbelieving must have their part in the lake that burneth with fire and brimstone."

I want to say before I close that God with all His omnipotence at His disposal never wastes anything. He never sends a flood if a shower will do; never sends a fortune if a shilling will do, never sends an army if a man will do. And He never thunders if a whisper will do.

He never works by miracles if He can achieve the same end by the instrumentality of natural laws. Your child lies sick. You ask God to heal him. If God can do so by whispering to your heart, or to the heart, it may be, of your physician, the secret balm for that particular malady, He will not work a special miracle for all your prayers. And if you are fool enough to say, "I don't want God's whispers; it must be thunder or nothing!" God will say: It shall be nothing.

He never gives special dreams, or voices, or visions, or revelations, if Scripture will do. Some people are for ever waiting for God, in some special providence, to speak to them of His grace or of His will. And He will never do it if He has already revealed His will to them in His Word. That Word is so plain that the one who runs may read. He will send no further revelation; but calls upon all people everywhere to repent and believe that Word. And what shall the end be of those who obey not the Gospel?"

F. W. Boreham, "The Whisper of God," *The Whisper of God and Other Sermons* (London: Arthur H. Stockwell, 1902), 9-23.

THE OTHER SIDE OF THE HILL

"But what is on *the other side of the hill?*"

That was the question. That is always the question. My friend and I had been spinning along in the car, the towering mountain and the shining harbor behind us, while each bend in the road presented us with a fresh unfolding of the ceaseless panorama of woodland, pasture, and stream. We were bound for nowhere, and so far as we could see the road led there. We were out for the pure sake of being out. All at once a sense of chilliness crept over us, and we were reminded that even the wealthiest days become bankrupt at last. Should we turn round and go home? There was only one objection. Right ahead of us lay a long range of hills. They had attracted our attention a few hours earlier as we sat under a big tree by the side of the road enjoying an alfresco lunch. During the afternoon their massive forms had crept nearer and nearer, as the car had sped swiftly towards them. They captivated our fancy and lured us on. There was something taunting and challenging about them.

'Shall we turn round and go home?'

'But, what is on the other side of the hill?'

That, I say, is the question. It is the oldest question in the world and the greatest question in the world. All the pathos and the tragedy of the ages are crammed into it. It was the first question that man asked; it will be the last that he will try to answer. Wherever on this planet you find a man, you find him with eyes turned wistfully towards the distant ranges, repeating to himself again and yet again the old, old question, 'The hill! The other side of the hill! What is on the other side of the hill?'

That is how history and geography—and everything else—came to be. The first man, toiling amid his weedy pastures, earned his bread in the sweat of his brow. But often, in the cool of the evening, he sat outside his primitive dwelling and pointed away to the hill tops that here and there broke the skyline. 'I wonder,' he said a hundred times to his companion, 'I wonder what is on the other side of the hill!' It never fell to his happy lot to sweep with delighted eye the valleys that stretched out beyond those ranges; but his sons and his grandsons conquered those tantalizing heights. They went out, north, south, east, and west; climbed one range and caught sight of another; were lured on and on—always by the old, old question; wandered beyond reach of each other; lost touch with the old home; settled here and settled there; and so your tribes, your races, your nations, and your empires came to be. It was the other side of the hill that did it.

And if it was the other side of the hill that made them, it was also the other side of the hill that made them great. For the great peoples have been the exploring peoples; and what is exploration but an attempt to discover the land that lies on the other side of the hill? Here, in Australia, exploration began with the conquest of the Blue Mountains. Settlement was confined to a narrow strip of land on the far east of the continent. And there, to the west, were the hills. And every evening, as shepherds and squatters watched the sun set over those huge, rugged peaks, they itched to discover what lay beyond the ranges. Again and again they attempted to solve the eternal secret; again and again they were baulked and defeated. Then came that never-to-be-forgotten day, a hundred years ago, when Blaxland, Lawson, and Wentworth crossed the mountains. They found that a great continent with fertile valleys, spreading plains, and rolling prairies lay on the other side of the hill. And on that memorable day the history of Australia began. It has been so everywhere. What was the opening up of America but the constant desire to discover what was on the other side of the hill? Think of that great moment—only twenty-one years after the epoch-making voyage of Columbus—when Vasco Nunez de Balboa

> With eagle eye
> First stared at the Pacific—and all his men
> Looked at each other with a wild surmise,
> Silent upon a peak in Darien.

Why the 'wild surmise'? Simply because they had found an ocean without looking for it! They were not searching for the Pacific; they were simply trying to find out what was on the other side of the hill! That was all.

Yes, that was all; and yet, after all, it is a fine thing to know what is on the other side of the hill. Who can read the fiery theological controversies of days gone by without wishing that each of the angry disputants had been able to peep over the brow of the ridge? Think of the language with which Luther and Calvin assailed each other! Think even of the correspondence of Wesley and Toplady. Wesley, the greatest evangelical force that England has ever known, wrote of the author of 'Rock of Ages,' 'Mr. Augustus Toplady I know well; but I do not fight with chimney-sweeps. He is too dirty a writer for me to meddle with; I should only foul my fingers.' Toplady was quite capable of repaying the founder of Methodism in his own coin. Wesley, he declared, was a hatcher of blasphemies; his forehead was impervious to a blush; he had perpetrated upon the public a known, a willful, and a palpable lie! But it is too bad of me to drag these amenities of eighteenth-century controversy from the dust that has so long covered them. Let me bury them again at once; and let us remember Wesley only as the greatest spiritual force in the making of modern England, and let us remember Toplady only as the author of our favorite hymn.

For, after all, what do these angry sentences prove? They only prove that, for a little season, neither Wesley nor Toplady were able to see what was on the other side of the hill. I never read a newspaper controversy, or listen to a heated debate, without feeling that. It is so obvious that each of the disputants is standing on his own side of the hill, shouting at his opponent over the ridge that separates them.

'The bush consists principally of *wattle!*' cries A., looking around him at the swaying tassels of gold.

'I tell you that the bush consists principally of *gum!*' replies B., as he hears the flapping of the great strips of bark on every side.

'It is *wattle!*' cries A.

'It is *gum!*' cries B.

'You're distorting the facts!' shrieks A.

'You are telling lies!' returns B. And so the quarrel goes on; both A. and B. getting hotter and angrier as it proceeds. But anybody who stands on the ridge, looking down into both valleys, can see that both are right. On A.'s side the soil and the general conditions favor the growth of the wattle, and the wattle undoubtedly predominates. Just over the hill, the eucalyptus is in its element, and, as a consequence, the blue-gum reigns without a rival there. If only A. and B. could each have taken a peep over the hilltop! If only Calvin could have seen things as they presented themselves to the eye of Luther; and if only Luther could have looked at the universe from Calvin's standpoint! If only Wesley could have taken Toplady by the arm, and they could have walked together—first to the one side of the hill and then to the other! If only all our controversialists could be convinced of the very obvious truth that a peak is the meeting-place of two separate valleys! But alas, alas; it is very difficult. So many people seem to suppose that a hilltop crowns one valley and one valley only. So few are willing to see what grows on the other side of the hill.

And yet, for the matter of that, every man knows what is on the other side of the hill. Immensity is on the other side of the hill. Infinity is on the other side of the hill. From my doorstep to the hilltop is a matter of a mile or two at the most; but who can measure in miles the land that lies on the other side of the hill? Between me and the hills lie a cluster of farms; but all the continents and oceans lie over the ranges—on the other side of the hill. Therein lies the consecration and the glory of the Church.

On a pinnacle in South America, at the very summit of a lofty range of mountains, an immense statue of Jesus was recently placed. There is a deeper significance in the incident than the sculptors themselves saw. For Christ is always on the hilltops pointing His Church to the immensities beyond. The Church has always inclined towards parochialism; she has contented herself with those few miles that lie between herself and the distant foothills. But the Master has stood ever on the sunlit summit pointing to the infinities beyond. It is the story of Kipling's 'Explorer':

> There's no sense in going further—it's the edge of cultivation!
> So they said, and I believed it—broke my land and sowed my crop—
> Built my barns and strung my fences on the little border station,
> Tucked away below the foothills where the trails run out and stop.
> Till a voice, as bad as conscience, rang interminable changes,
> On one everlasting whisper, day and night repeated—so:
> 'Something hidden! Go and find it! Go and look behind the ranges!
> Something lost behind the ranges! Lost, and waiting for You—GO!'

'Go,' said the Master. 'Go ye into all the world.' In that tremendous 'Go,' the Church has caught a glimpse of the other side of the hill, and has herself been saved from narrowness by the discovery.

Yes, immensity and infinity are on the other side of the hill. Immensity and Infinity—and Eternity. That is why the pilgrims of the ages have been struggling with bleeding feet up those precipitous slopes. They hoped that, from the summit, they might catch one satisfying glimpse of the Beyond. Sages and savages alike have gazed with awe at the hilltops, wondering what lay on the other side. No tribe or people has ever been discovered but in some tent or wigwam or kraal there dwelt some priest or fakir or medicineman who guessed and muttered of the things on the other side of the hill. Oh, the witchery and the mystery of the other side of the hill! Oh, the lure and the fascination of the other side of the hill! There is, I say, a deeper significance in that South American statue than its constructors imagined. For Jesus stands on the hilltop. He sees what is on our side of the hill, and He sees what is on the other. And, since *He knows,* I need no fakir, no guesser, no medicine-man. He has brought life and immortality to light through the gospel. And there He stands! And so long as He commands that eminence, there is no terror for me on either side of the hill.

F. W. Boreham, "The Other Side of the Hill," *The Other Side of the Hill* (London: Charles H. Kelly, 1917), 39-47.

FYODOR DOSTOYEVSKY'S TEXT

I

Russia had never seen such a funeral. It was in many respects the most extraordinary demonstration of public feeling ever witnessed in the Czar's dominions. The sorrow was a national sorrow, the loftiest and the lowliest alike lamented; the cities were in tears. Forty thousand men followed the coffin to the grave. 'When I heard of Dostoyevsky's death,' says Tolstoy, 'I felt that I had lost a kinsman, the closest and the dearest, and the one of whom I had most need.' The students of Russia, to whom he had been a father, sent an open letter to his widow.

'Dostoyevsky's ideals,' they said, 'will never be forgotten. From generation to generation we shall hand them down as a precious inheritance from our great and beloved teacher. His memory will never be extinguished in the hearts of the youth of Russia, and, in years to come, we shall teach our children to love and honor his name. Dostoyevsky will always stand out brightly before us in the battle of life; for it was he who taught us the possibility of preserving the purity of the soul undefiled in every position of life and in all conceivable conditions and circumstances.'

Clearly, then, we have here a man among men; a man who stirred the hearts of thousands; a man who, through his books, still speaks to multitudes. What is the secret of his deep and widespread influence? Let us go back a day or two!

II

That never-to-be-forgotten funeral took place on February 12, 1881. On February 9, Dostoyevsky lay dying. 'When he awoke that morning,' his daughter tells us, 'my mother realized that his hours were numbered.'

Brave little mother! so this is the end of her fifteen years of romance! In the novels of Dostoyevsky there is no prettier story than the story of the meeting of these two. Dostoyevsky was forty-five at the time. Through voluntarily taking over the debts of his dead brother, his finances had become involved. Moreover, he had fallen into the clutches of an unscrupulous publisher, for whom he had contracted to write a novel on the understanding that, if it was not finished by a certain date, all the author's copyrights would fall into the publisher's hands. As the date approached, the impossibility of the task became evident, and ruin stared him in the face. Somebody advised him to get a stenographer; but no stenographer could be found.

There was, it is true, a girl of nineteen who knew shorthand; but lady stenographers were then unknown; and the girl doubted if her people would consent to her taking the appointment. However, Dostoyevsky's fame removed the parents' scruples, and she set to work. On her way to the novelist's house, she used to tell her daughter afterwards, she tried to imagine what their first session would be like. 'We shall work for an hour,' she thought, 'and then we shall talk of literature.' Dostoyevsky had had an epileptic attack the night before; he was absent-minded, nervous, and peremptory. He seemed quite unconscious of the charms of his young stenographer, and treated her as a kind of Remington typewriter. He dictated the first chapter of his novel in a harsh voice, complained that she did not write fast enough, made her read aloud what he had dictated, scolded her, and declared that she had not understood him. She was crushed, and left the house determined never to return. But she thought better of it during the night, and, next morning, resumed her post. Little by little, Dostoyevsky became conscious that his Remington machine was a charming young girl and an ardent admirer of his genius. He confided his troubles to her and she pitied him. In her girlish dream, she had pictured him petted and pampered; instead, she saw a sick man, weary, badly fed, badly lodged, badly served, hunted down like a wild beast by merciless creditors, and ruthlessly exploited by selfish relatives. She perceived the idea of protecting Dostoyevsky, of hating the heavy burden he had taken upon his shoulders, and of comforting him in his sorrows. She was not in love with this man, who was more than twenty-five years her senior, but she understood his beautiful soul and reverenced his genius. She determined to save Dostoyevsky from his publishers, and succeeded. She begged him to prolong the hours of dictation, spent the night copying out what she had taken down in the day, and worked with such good-will that, to the chagrin of the avaricious publisher, the novel was ready on the appointed day. And, shortly afterwards, he married her.

And now, fifteen years afterwards—the funeral was on the anniversary of the wedding—Dostoyevsky is dying!

'He made us come into the room,' his daughter says, 'and, taking our little hands in his, he begged my mother to read the *Parable of the Prodigal Son*. He listened with his eyes closed, absorbed in his thoughts. "My children," he said in his feeble voice, "never forget what you have just heard. Have absolute faith in God and never despair of His pardon. I love you dearly, but my love is nothing compared with the love of God for all those He has created. Even if you should be so unhappy as to commit a crime in the course of your life, never despair of God. You are His children; humble yourselves before Him, as before your father, implore His pardon, and He will rejoice over your repentance, as the father rejoiced over that of the *Prodigal Son*." '

A few minutes later Dostoyevsky passed triumphantly away. 'I have been present,' says Aimee Dostoyevsky, 'at many deathbeds, but none was so radiant as that of my father. He saw without fear the end approaching. His was a truly Christian death. He was ready to appear before his Eternal Father hoping that, to recompense him for all that he had suffered in this life, God would give him another great work to do, another great task to accomplish.'

III

Now before we turn on tiptoe from this silent room, let us examine, reverently and carefully, the faded and battered New Testament lying at the dead man's side—the Testament from which, a few moments ago, the mother read in brave but broken accents the story of the *Prodigal Son*. It has a history; and that history may reveal much of what we wish to know.

For this man, who has just died so restfully, has looked death in the face before. His career is as romantic as his novels; indeed, his novels are, in the main, a reflection of his career. As a small boy he revels in historical romances—particularly those of Sir Walter Scott—and he enters so vividly into the thrilling experiences of the various characters that he often faints with the volume clasped in his hands. He is fond, too, of the open air. 'All my life,' he says, 'I have loved the forest, with its mushrooms, its fruits, its insects, its birds, and its squirrels; I reveled in the scent of its damp leaves. Even at this moment, as I write, I can smell the aroma of the birches.' As a young fellow, he interests himself in the welfare of his country; he joins a society that meets to discuss public questions; and, at the age of twenty-eight, is arrested for meddling with such matters. With thirty-three others he is charged with conspiracy, and, after a hurried trial, is sentenced to death. The condemned men afterwards discover that the sentence was a grim jest on the part of the Czar and his lieutenants, who thought, by this expedient, to frighten them.

On a bitter morning, with the temperature many degrees below freezing point, they are led to the scaffold;

their ordinary clothes are exchanged for shrouds; and thus, nearly naked, they are compelled to stand for half an hour while the burial service is being slowly read. Facing them, stand the soldiers with their muskets. A pile of coffins is stacked suggestively in a corner of the yard. At the last moment, with the muskets actually at the shoulders of the guards, a white flag is waved, and it is announced that the Czar has commuted the sentence to one of ten years' exile in Siberia. Several of the prisoners lost their reason under the strain; several others died shortly afterwards. Dostoyevsky passed courageously through the ordeal; but it affected his nerves; he never recalled the experience without a shudder, and he refers to it with horror in several of his books.

On Christmas Eve, 1848, he commenced the dreadful journey to Omsk, and remained in Siberia 'like a man buried alive, nailed down in his coffin.' On his arrival in that desolate region, two women slip a New Testament into his hand, and, taking advantage of a moment when the officer's back is turned, whisper to him to search it carefully at his leisure. Between the pages he finds a note for twenty-five rubles. The money is a vast comfort to him: but the New Testament itself proves an infinitely vaster one.

His daughter tells us that, during his exile, that Testament was his only solace. 'He studied the precious volume from cover to cover; pondered every word; learned much of it by heart; and never forgot it. All his works are saturated with it, and it is this which gives them their power. Many of his admirers have said to me that it was a strange chance that ordained that my father should have only the gospels to read during the most important and formative years of his life. But was it a chance? Is there such a thing as chance in our lives? The work of Jesus is not finished; in each generation He chooses His disciples, signs to them to follow Him, and gives them the same power over the human heart that He gave to the poor fishermen of Galilee.' Aimee Dostoyevsky believed that it was by that divine hand that the Testament was presented to her father that day. 'Throughout his life,' she adds, 'he would never be without his old prison Testament, the faithful friend that had consoled him in the darkest hours of his life. He always took it with him on his travels and kept it in a drawer of his writing-table, within reach of his hand. He consulted it in all the important moments of his life,' and, as we have seen, it was his comfort in the hour of death.

IV

It was in Siberia that Dostoyevsky discovered the beauty of the *Parable of the Prodigal Son*. Siberia was the far country. It was there that he saw the prodigal among the husks and the swine. His companions were the lowest of the low and the vilest of the vile. 'Imagine,' he says, 'an old crazy wooden building that should long ago have been broken up as useless. In the summer it is unbearably hot, in the winter unbearably cold. All the boards are rotten. On the ground filth lies an inch thick; every instant one is in danger of slipping. The small windows are so frozen over that even by day one can scarcely read; the ice on the panes is three inches thick. We are packed like herrings in a barrel. The atmosphere is intolerable; the prisoners stink like pigs; there are vermin by the bushel; we sleep upon bare boards.' And, in the midst of this disgusting and degrading scene, I catch a glimpse of Dostoyevsky. At first glance he is by no means an attractive figure. He is small and slender, round-shouldered and thick-necked. He is clothed in convict motley, one leg black, the other gray; the colors of his coat likewise divided; his head half-shaved and bent forward in deep thought. His face is half the face of a Russian peasant and half the face of a dejected criminal. He is shy, taciturn, rather ugly, and extremely awkward. He has a flattened nose; small piercing eyes under eyelashes which tremble with nervousness; and a long thick untidy beard with fair hair. The stamp of his epilepsy is distinctly upon him. We see all this at a glance, and the glance is not alluring. But Nekrassov, the poet, has given us the picture as the convicts saw it. In this picture Dostoyevsky appears almost sublime. He moves among his fellow-prisoners with his New Testament in his hand, telling them its stories and reading to them its words of comfort and grace. He seems to them a kind of prophet, gently rebuking their blasphemies and excesses, and speaking to them of poetry, of science, of God, and of the love of Christ. It is his way of pointing the prodigal to the path that leads to the Father's heart and the Father's home.

V

For this was the treasure that he found in that New Testament! This was the beauty of the story of *The Prodigal Son!* It revealed the way to the Father. 'One sees the truth more clearly when one is unhappy,' he writes from Siberia. 'And yet God gives me moments of perfect peace; in such moments I love and believe that I am loved; in such moments I have formulated my creed, wherein all is clear

and holy to me. This Creed is extremely simple: here it is.
I believe that there is nothing lovelier, deeper, more sympathetic, more rational, more manly, and more perfect than
the Savior; I say to myself with jealous love that not only
is there no one else like Him, but that there *could* be no
one. I would even say more; if anyone could prove to me
that Christ is outside the truth, and if the truth really did
exclude Christ, I should prefer to stay with Christ and not
with truth.' Alexander Puschkin has a poem about a poor
knight who, in a moment of supreme exaltation, sees the
Holy Virgin at the foot of the Cross. Dostoyevsky was very
fond of the poem; whenever he read it, his face was radiated,
his voice trembled, his eyes filled with tears. 'For it was,'
his daughter says, 'the story of his own soul. He, too, was a
poor knight; he, too, had a beatific vision; but it was not the
medieval Virgin who appeared to him but Christ who came
to him in his prison and called him to follow Him.'

> *Christ—no one like Christ!*
> *Christ—the Savior!*
> *Christ—the way to the Father!*

On his bended knees Dostoyevsky blessed God for
sending him into the Siberian steppes. For it was amid
those stern and awful solitudes that he found the road that
leads to the Father's home.

VI

That old prison Testament, and the revelation that it
brought to him, were in his thoughts through all the years
that followed. We catch fitful glimpses of the battered

volume in all his writings. I pick up *The Possessed,* and I find, near the close of the book, as the story draws to its climax, that Stepan Trofimovitch is taken ill and Sofya Matveyevna sits by his couch, reading. And what is she reading? She is reading two striking passages from the New Testament!

And in *Crime and Punishment* there is a really tremendous scene. In his article on Dostoyevsky in the *Encyclopedia Britannica,* Mr. Thomas Seccombe, M.A., declares that, for poignancy and emotional intensity, there is nothing in modern literature to equal it. It describes Raskolnikoff, the conscience-stricken and self-tormented murderer, creeping at dead of night to the squalid waterside hovel in which Sonia lives. Sonia is part of the flotsam and jetsam of the city's wreckage. The relationship between these two was a relationship of sympathy; each had sinned terribly; and each had sinned for the sake of others rather than for self. On a rickety little table in Sonia's room stands a tallow candle fixed in an improvised candlestick of twisted metal. In the course of earnest conversation, Sonia glances at a book lying on a chest of drawers. He takes it down. It is a New Testament. He hands it to Sonia and begs her to read it to him. 'Sonia opens the book; her hands tremble; the words stick in her throat. Twice she tries without being able to utter a syllable.' At length she succeeds. And then—

'She closes the book: she seems afraid to raise her eyes on Raskolnikoff: her feverish trembling continues. The dying piece of candle dimly lights up this low-ceilinged room in which an assassin and a harlot have just read the Book of Books!'

This is in the middle of the story. On the last page, when Raskolnikoff and Sonia have both been purified by suffering, Raskolnikoff is still cherishing in his prison cell the New Testament which, at his earnest request, Sonia has brought him.

Here is Raskolnikoff—a Prodigal Son!

Here is Sonia—a Prodigal Daughter!

Here is the Book of Books pointing the prodigals to the Father's House!

The candle in Sonia's wretched room burned lower and lower, and at last sputtered out. But the candle that, in that Siberian prison, was lit in Dostoyevsky's soul, grew taller and taller the longer it burned. Like the path of the just, which shineth more and more unto the perfect day, its light waxed brighter and clearer. It flung its radiance right around the world: it found a reflection in the glowing lives of thousands; it lit up Dostoyevsky's death chamber with the glory of a great hope; and it illumined his flight to that Celestial City in which they need neither candle nor sun.

F. W. Boreham, "Fyodor Dostoyevsky's Text," *A Faggot of Torches* (London: The Epworth Press, 1926), 94-106.

A PROPHET'S PILGRIMAGE

Jonah fascinates me. He stands with Bunyan and Newton and Brainerd among my spiritual masters. There was a time when I was interested in Jonah's adventure with the whale, just as there was a time when I was interested in Bunyan's adventure with the press-gang, Newton's adventure with the slave-ship and Brainerd's adventures among Red Indians. But, of late years, things have assumed a more just perspective. As in the cases of Bunyan, Newton and Brainerd, I find myself thrilled by the epic struggle in the prophet's soul. The real romance of Jonah is the stirring romance of his spiritual pilgrimage.

I

The tragedy in the soul of this passionate and impulsive young prophet lay in the fact that he had a God a million sizes too small for him—a God whose littleness failed to fit the immensities of his own intricate and immeasurable personality, a God who could not inhabit and furnish and occupy the spacious apartments of his mind and heart and soul.

It is very interesting to trace the evolution of the conception of God in the infancy of the race. It is clear that Man set out on the assumption that God was a mere magnified man, of human piques and manlike passions, of limited power and local habitation, a Ghostly Human whom he openly worshipped but secretly distrusted and dreaded. Men began with a microscopic deity. He was essentially little and therefore essentially local. Cain's tiny conception of God led him to the conclusion that a few days' pilgrimage would carry him, not only out of sight of his deity, but altogether beyond the territorial limits within which that deity had power to protect him. Jacob thought of God as one who could lend Himself to trickery, and, perhaps, Himself be deceived. And, as a natural consequence, he thought of God as reigning only within very narrow geographic boundaries. It came upon him as a staggering surprise that, in his fugitive flight, he had not evaded the vigilant care of Jehovah. So was it with Jonah. Jonah cherished the conception of a small God of changing moods and fickle fancies, a God who might easily be turned from His purpose by a people's sorrow or a prophet's pique. And, therefore, and as a natural consequence, he thought of God as a local deity, who could readily be evaded by the simple expedient of crossing the sea. From the deck of the gallant vessel of Tarshish he waved a confident good-bye to the God whom he had left behind him.

The greatest day in a man's life is the day on which he finds himself overwhelmed and bowed to earth by a sense of the greatness of God; the day on which, like Isaiah, he sees the Lord high and lifted up, His train filling the temple; the day on which he feels that God is everything and everywhere, filling all things and inhabiting eternity; the day on which he sees other things only as they relate themselves to Him—the clouds the dust of His feet and the stars the gems of His crown.

But that day had not yet dawned upon Jonah. Jonah's God was a small God. Jonah was the servant of God, yet did not know the God whose servant he was! He was the prophet of the Most High, yet did not know the Most High as the Most High! He was the missionary of Jehovah, yet did not know Jehovah! In such appalling conditions some irretrievable spiritual disaster was inevitable. And, very swiftly, it swooped down upon him.

II

For the person who cherishes a tiny conception of *God* must, of necessity, harbor a cramped and unworthy conception of *the Kingdom of God.*

'*Arise, go to Nineveh,*' came the call. It was a sublime opportunity for a magnificent and heroic adventure. A hundred books have since been written telling of thrilling exploits and hair-breadth escapes on that romantic road that runs down from Jerusalem to Nineveh. To many a man the chance of spending crowded hours of glorious life amid the bandits and Bedouins of that eastern road would have seemed the lure of a golden destiny. But not to Jonah. Nineveh! Nineveh! Jonah thought of Nineveh, that great heathen city, with its stately palaces, its lofty towers, its splendid temples, its abounding wealth, its teeming population; but he could find no place for Nineveh within the kingdom of his dreams. The kingdom of God, to him, consisted of Israel—only that and nothing more. So, hearing the call, he sadly shook his head, turned away in disdain, and fled from the presence of the Lord who called him.

And when thus he shook his head, and turned away, he proved that he was out of touch with all that is best in God and with all that is best in man.

For the thing that we love to contemplate in our thought of God is the thought of His catholicity.

For the love of God is broader
Than the measures of man's mind,
And the heart of the Eternal
Is most wonderfully kind.

A moment or two ago we traced the evolution of truth in the *Old* Testament. The evolution of truth in the *New* Testament is very similar. It is the gradual revelation of the worldwide sympathies and boundless love of the Savior of men. He was always bursting the bonds of prejudice, and shattering the pitiful parochialisms that His racial and social environments sought with cruel persistence to impose upon Him. He is always hungry for the world—the whole, wide world. And the revelation of His risen glory reaches its glowing climax with an apocalyptic vision of surpassing splendor; a vision of the City Four-square; a city in which there is room for the inhabitants of countless worlds; a city in which the seer sees the Savior surrounded by a multitude that no man can number, a throng that no statistician can count! But, with all this, Jonah was hopelessly out of touch.

And he was equally out of touch with all that is best in men. For there is nothing in any man finer than his interest in all men. Each individual is moved by a great race-consciousness. The most typical spectacle on the planet is a man with a newspaper in his hand. Morning and evening, every man wants to know the fates and fortunes, the dooms and destinies, of all other men. For, unlike the beasts that perish, man is conscious of a life infinitely larger than the life of the individual. He cherishes a gregarianism of an ampler kind than any known in the wilds. Wolves may go in packs, birds in flocks and deer in herds; but the life of each of these aggregations is independent of, and often in rivalry with, the life of each similar company. The pack binds a few wolves in one: but there is no tie that embraces universal wolfhood. Each *man,* however, feels that all men belong to him. Each settlement feels itself to be part and parcel of every distant city. The individual wants the world; and his appetite for the world expresses itself in his insatiable thirst for news. But with all this—and it is this that has moved man to his most splendid triumphs and adventures—Jonah threw himself out of touch as, with a glance towards Nineveh, he turned sadly away.

You may always suspect your faith when it becomes exclusive. When a man can find room for Jerusalem within the compass of his sympathy, but can find no room for Nineveh, he may take it as a symptom that his soul is sick. His spiritual life is unhealthy. True spirituality is magnificently inclusive. What is it that Edward Markham sings?

> He drew a circle that shut me out—
> Heretic, rebel, a thing to flout;
> But Love and I had the wit to win;
> We drew a circle that took Him in

Jeff Kilbourne was a young citizen of the United States who happened to be studying art in Paris when the War broke out. He felt the thrill of the stirring movements by which he was encircled, and longed to have some part in them. Yet how could he? He could not return to America to enlist, and, anyhow, the United States had not, at that stage, entered the field of hostilities. So he joined a French battalion and soon became the most popular member of it. Everybody loved Jeff. His comrades would have laid down their lives for him; the people of the village in which the regiment was quartered became wonderfully fond of him; the old priest felt strangely drawn to Jeff, and was always the happier after catching his smile. But one day the company was sent into action and most of its members fell— including Jeff. Next day the old priest was called upon to bury the dead in the graveyard beside the church and then a serious complication arose. For what about Jeff? Jeff was a Protestant; how could he be buried with his comrades in Catholic ground? The good old priest was full of grief; but he saw no way out of the difficulty. He did the best he could by arranging that the men should be buried in rows across the graveyard—rows that stretched from wall to wall—and that Jeff should be buried in one of those rows but just outside the wall. He would thus be in the company of his comrades; the wall alone intervening. The burial took place, and the old priest, weary with his labors, returned to his well-earned rest. But that night the villagers arose in the moonlight and, joined by Jeff's surviving comrades, they pulled down part of the wall and rebuilt it in such a way that it took Jeff in! It is a great thing when we pull down our narrow walls and make them more inclusive. The religion that takes in Jerusalem, and leaves out Nineveh, the religion that takes in Great Britain and leaves out India or China, is no religion at all. I need a faith that takes in not only Europe and America and Australia, but Asia and Africa and all the countless islands of the Seven Seas. But at this point Jonah's faith collapsed. He had a small conception of God, and, as an inevitable consequence, he had a small conception of the *Kingdom of God.*

III

And, just as inevitably, the man who cherishes a small conception of *God,* and a small conception of *the Kingdom of God,* can have but *a small gospel* to preach. How can he possibly have a great one?

'*Yet forty days and Nineveh shall be overthrown!*' Who would care to be the preacher of such a gospel? I seem to see this hot-hearted and hot-headed young prophet—tall, lithe, sinewy, with earnest face, flashing eyes and long black beard—as he rushes from one central point in Nineveh to another. 'These domes shall crash,' he cries, almost in exultation, 'these towers shall totter; these palaces shall fall; these people shall die like flies in the streets!' It is a poor, poor gospel; a small, narrow, vindictive gospel. Yet, with so small a *God,* and so small a conception of *the Kingdom of God,* how can he proclaim a nobler one?

IV

It all came right in the end; and it came right because Jonah made two startling and sensational discoveries. He discovered something in his fellowmen that he had never previously suspected, and he discovered something in God that he had never suspected before.

He discovered in his fellowmen an amazing susceptibility to the approach of divine truth. Mr. Wesley used to say that three stupendous surprises awaited him in heaven. He would be surprised to see so many there whom he had never expected to find in the Celestial City; he would be surprised to find so many absent whom he had confidently expected to meet; and he would be most of all surprised to find that he himself had reached heaven after all!

Most ministers are confronted by *two* astonishments; they are often amazed at finding apathy where they looked for sympathy, and they are just as often surprised at finding such real concern where they had only looked for abject indifference.

Jonah's *first* surprise met him alike on sea and on land. He preached to the sailors on the ship, and those heathen seamen were soon upon their knees in contrition and supplication! He preached to the citizens of Nineveh, and, from the king downwards, they repented in sackcloth and ashes!

Jonah had no idea, until then, that, in the depths of the human soul, there is a certain something that responds to the divine appeal as a lock responds to the key that is made to fit it.

And his *second* discovery? His second discovery was more sensational still: He made his second discovery when he saw God relent towards the people of Nineveh and regard their cry for forgiveness.

Why, he asked himself, why did God give the men of Nineveh another chance? And then it occurred to him that the thing that had happened to Nineveh was exactly the thing that had happened to *him*. For he, a prodigal prophet, flying from the presence of the Lord, had been brought back and given a second chance. 'The word of the Lord came unto Jonah *a second time*.' Why did God give a second chance to Nineveh—and to him? And then the truth flashed upon him. Of course! There could be but one explanation. God must *love* Nineveh! God must *love* Jonah! He had never thought of that. It had never occurred to him that God was very fond even of the men who had never heard of Him, very fond of the men who were sinning against Him, very fond even of the prophets who, rather than do His bidding, were shamefully flying from His presence.

Those two discoveries made a new man of Jonah. That is why, centuries later, Jesus talked about Jonah, talked wistfully and kindly and appreciatively about him. We may leave it at that. And, leaving it at that, we leave Jonah in good company. Jonah and Jesus! Jesus and Jonah! Jonah emerging from his weird and watery tomb to call a great city to repentance; Jesus rising from His grave among the lilies to be the Savior of the whole wide world; and both of them pointing mutely to the lands beyond the horizon— the kingdoms that by every right must become the kingdoms of our God and of His Christ.

F. W. Boreham, "A Prophet's Pilgrimage," *A Witch's Brewing* (London: The Epworth Press, 1932), 160-162.

THE POWDER MAGAZINE

I

I have a special fondness for explosive people. I can never persuade myself that dynamite got into the world by accident. I intolerantly discount the theory that the devil built all the volcanoes, and that his minions feed their furious fires. I have admired an indescribable grandeur in the hurricane. I have felt the cyclone to be splendid, and the tornado to be next door to sublimity. Even the earthquake has a glory of its own. And how a thunderstorm clears the air! How deliciously sweet my garden smells when the riven clouds have passed, and the glittering drops are still clinging like pendant gems to the drooping petals and the bright green leaves! And, in the same way, I have discovered something terribly sublime in those stormy elements that sweep the realm within.

There was a time when my eyes were closed to this side of the glory of God's world. I used to think it a dreadful thing for Paul to be cross with Barnabas. I thought it shocking if Barnabas spoke sharply to Paul. For Barnabas was 'a good man and full of the Holy Ghost.' And Paul was 'a good man and full of the Holy Ghost.' And I thought that so lovely and tranquil a little world had no room for dynamite. Till, one day, a thing happened that made me feel as though a volcano had burst into eruption at my feet! I was thunderstruck! The circumstances are briefly told. Paul and Barnabas had just completed one adventurous, triumphant, and historic campaign together. Together they had crossed the tumbling seas in crazy little vessels that would scarcely now be permitted to cruise about a river. Together they had trudged, singing as they went, along the lonely forest trail through the lowlands of Pamphylia. Together they had climbed the great pass over the mountains of Pisidia. Together they had felt the exhilaration of the heights as they surveyed, shading their eyes with their hands, the lands that they had come to conquer. Together, at the risk of their lives, they had forded streams in full tumultuous flood; together they had known hunger and thirst; together they had shared unspeakable hardships; together they had faced the most terrible privations. Together they had been deified one day, and together they had been stoned the next. Together they had made known the love of Christ in the great capitals; together they had rejoiced over their converts; and then, together, they had made that never-to-be-forgotten return journey. I have often tried to imagine their emotions, as, on the homeward way, they came in sight of one city after another that they had visited in coming. In coming, those cities were heathen capitals and nothing more. In returning, there were churches there and fond familiar faces! And what meetings those must have been in each city when the members again welcomed Paul and Barnabas; when the two scarred heroes told the thrilling tale of their experiences elsewhere; and when, in each church, ministers and officers were appointed! And, leaving a chain of thoroughly organized churches behind them across the land, as a ship leaves her foaming wake across the waters, the two valiant and dauntless companions returned home. How all this had welded these two noble souls together! They are knit, each to each, like the souls of David and Jonathan.

And now a second campaign is suggested. Barnabas proposes that they should take with them Mark. Mark, who was the nephew of Barnabas had started with them on their former journey; but, at the first brush of persecution, he had hastily scampered home. Paul instantly vetoes the proposal. He will not hear of it. He will not have a coward at any price. His soul loathes a traitor. Barnabas insists, but Paul remains adamant. 'And the contention was so sharp between them that they departed asunder the one from the other,' and, probably, never met again. If I had not been actually present and witnessed this amazing explosion with my own eyes, I fancy my faith would have staggered. As it is, the surprising spectacle only taught me that God has left room for dynamite in a world like this; and, much as I admired both Paul and Barnabas before the outburst, I loved them still more when the storm was past.

II

I have said that I saw this astonishing outburst with my own eyes. That is so, or at least so I fancied. For it seemed to me that I was honored with a seat on a committee of which both Paul and Barnabas were valued and revered members.

We all loved them, and treasured every gracious word that
fell from their lips. For 'Barnabas was a good man and full
of the Holy Ghost.' And 'Paul was a good man and full
of the Holy Ghost.' Now Mark had applied to the committee for engagement as a missionary. And Barnabas rose
to move his appointment. I shall never forget the charm
and grace with which he did it. I could see at a glance that
the good man was speaking under deep feeling. His voice
reflected his strong emotion. He reminded us that Mark
was his relative, and he felt a certain heavy responsibility
for his nephew's spiritual well-being. He trembled, he said,
lest he should be condemned as one who risked his life for
the heathen over the seas, but who displayed no serious
solicitude concerning his own kith and kin. He had wept
in secret over his young kinsman's former treachery. But it
had made him the more eager to win his soul in spite of
everything. He was alarmed lest the rejection of his relative
should lead to his utter humiliation, total exclusion, and
final loss. He admitted with shame and grief all that could
be alleged against him. He had been weighed in the balances
and found wanting. He had turned his back in the hour of
peril. But what of that? Had we not all our faults and fail-
ures? I remember that, as he said this, Barnabas glanced
round the council-table, and looked inquiringly into each
face. There was moisture in his own bright eyes, and each
man hung his head beneath that searching glance.

And then, he went on, surely there was something
admirable in Mark's original venture. He had nothing to
gain by going. It was his enthusiasm for the cause of Christ
that prompted him to go. It proved that his heart was in
the right place. And the very fact that he was anxious to set
out again, with a full knowledge of the perils before him,

proved indisputably that he had sincerely repented of his earlier unfaithfulness, and was eager for an opportunity of redeeming his name from contempt. How could we ourselves hope for forgiveness unless we were prepared to show mercy in a case like this? Once more those searchlights swept the faces round the table. And then, with wonderful tenderness, Barnabas reminded us of the bruised reed that must not be broken and of the smoking flax that must not be quenched. And, in the name of Him who, after His resurrection, found a special place for Peter, the disciple who had thrice denied his Lord, Barnabas implored us to favor his nephew's application. There was a hush in the room when the gracious speech was finished. We all felt that Barnabas was a good man and full of the Holy Ghost.

III

Then Paul rose. One could see at a glance that his whole soul rebelled against having to oppose the partner of so many providential escapes, the comrade of so many gallant fights. The affection of these two for each other was very beautiful. Paul admitted frankly that he had been deeply touched by the gracious words that had fallen from the lips of Barnabas. His heart leaped up to greet every one of those appeals. Each argument met with its echo and response in every fiber of his being. For old friendship's sake he would dearly like to accede to the request of Barnabas. Was it not through the influence of Barnabas, and in face of strong opposition, that he himself was admitted to the sacred service? And because Mark was his old friend's nephew he would especially wish to entertain the proposal. But we were gathered together, he reminded us, in the sacred interests of the kingdom of Christ. And for the sake of the honor of that kingdom we must be prepared to set aside considerations of friendship, and even to ignore the tender claims of kinship. The friendship of Barnabas was one of earth's most precious treasures; but he could not allow even that to influence him in a matter in which he felt that the integrity of the cause of Christ was at stake. The relatives of Barnabas were as dear to him as his own kith and kin; but there were higher considerations than domestic considerations. Mark had once—perhaps twice—proved himself unequal to the claims of this perilous undertaking. He might render excellent and valuable service in some other capacity. But for this particular enterprise, which required, as well as a warm heart, a cool head and a steady nerve, Mark was clearly unfitted. He became terror-stricken in the hour of danger. They could not afford to run such risks. A defection in their own party gave the enemy cause to blaspheme. It exposed them to ridicule and contempt. The heathen cried out that these men were prepared to follow Christ so long as Christ never went near a cross. The Jews, who had themselves suffered for their faith, laughed at a new doctrine from which its very teachers might be scared and intimidated. And the young converts would find it immensely more difficult to endure persecution for the gospel's sake if they beheld one of the missionaries turn his back in the hour of peril. He had long ago forgiven Mark, he said, for his former failure. Indeed, he scarcely recognized any need for forgiveness. He felt sorry for his young friend at the time, and he felt sorry for him still. Mark was a gentle spirit, not made for riots and tumults; and, in the shock of opposition, he was easily frightened. His love for Christ, and his zeal for service, were very admirable; and they all loved him for his simplicity and sincerity and enthusiasm. But, knowing his peculiar frailty, they must not expose either him or the cause to needless risk. The welfare of Mark, and the reputation of the Cross, were very dear to him; and he would on no account whatever agree to submit the delicate soul of Mark to a strain that it had already proved itself unable to bear, or the gospel to an unnecessary risk of being brought into disfavor and contempt. He implored the committee to deal wisely and considerately with the subtle and delicate and complex character of his young friend, and to prize above everything else the honor of the gospel. Personally he was quite determined that it would be a wicked and unjust and unkind thing to expose the soul of Mark to such imminent peril, and the Cross of Christ to such grave risk of further scandal. He would on no account take Mark. The speech was so tempered with tenderness, as well as with firmness and wisdom, that it created a profound impression. We all felt that Paul was a good man and full of the Holy Ghost.

IV

Neither would yield. How could they? Each had heard a voice that was higher and more imperative than the voice of sentiment or of friendship. It is ridiculous to say that they should have 'made it up' for old sake's sake, or for the gospel's sake, or for any other sake. Barnabas believed, in the very soul of him, that it would be wrong to leave Mark behind. And Paul believed, in the very soul of him, that it would be wrong to take Mark with them. You cannot bridge a gulf like that. Each tried to convince the other.

The contention became sharp but futile. And they parted. And I, for one, honor them. They could not, as 'good men and full of the Holy Ghost,' have done anything else. I do not pretend to understand why God has made room in the world for earthquakes and volcanoes. I see them tear up the valleys and hurl down the mountains; and I stand bewildered and astonished. But there they are! I do not pretend to understand these other explosive forces. But there they are! And I, for one, love both Paul and Barnabas the more that they will neither of them sacrifice, even for friendship's sweet sake, the interests of the cause of Christ.

In my New Zealand days I knew two men, almost aged. I have told the story in detail in *Mushrooms on the Moor.* These two men had been bosom friends. Time after time, year after year, they had walked up to the house of God in company. In the days of gray hairs they came to differ on important religious questions, and could no longer conscientiously worship beneath the same roof. They met; they tried to discuss the debatable doctrine; but their hearts were too full. Side by side they walked for miles along lonely roads on a clear, frosty, moonlight night, in the hope that presently a discussion would be possible. I walked in reverent silence some distance ahead of them. But speech never came. Grief had completely paralyzed the vocal powers, and the eyes were streaming with another eloquence. They wrung each other's hands at length, and parted without even a 'Good-night.' They still differ; they still occasionally meet; they still love. They even admire each other for being willing to sacrifice old fellowship for conscience sake. There is something here with which the more flippant advocates of church union do not reckon. Paul and

Barnabas are good men, both of them, and full of the Holy Ghost. But they cannot agree. Face to face, the contention becomes very sharp. They wisely part. As I say, I do not pretend to understand why God left so many explosive forces lying about His world; but there they are!

V

It all turned out wonderfully well, as it was bound to do. Barnabas, whatever became of him, made a hero of Mark. He became perfectly lion-hearted. 'Bring Mark with thee,' wrote Paul to Timothy, when he himself was awaiting his martyr-death at Rome. 'Bring Mark with thee, for he is profitable to me for my ministry.' And I like to think that when Peter felt that the time had come to put on permanent record the holy memories of earlier Galilean days, he employed Mark to pen the precious pamphlet for him. Peter and Mark understood each other. And as they worked together on that second 'gospel,' they had many a tearful talk of the way in which, long before, they had each played the coward's part, and had each been greatly forgiven and graciously restored. To those of us who look up to Paul and Barnabas as to a terrific height above us, it is splendid to know that there is room for Peter and for Mark in the heart that loves and in the service that ennobles.

F. W. Boreham, "The Powder Magazine," *The Other Side of the Hill* (London: Charles H. Kelly, 1917), 253-264.

OUR INTERRUPTIONS

Interruptions are extremely vexatious; but, when all is said and done, it is by our interruptions that we reach our goals. I have the highest scientific authority for saying that it is the interruption that really matters. I am writing on the fiftieth anniversary of the invention of the cablegram; and the cablegram is the fruit of deliberate and systematic interruption. The story of Samuel Morse, the genius to whom we owe the introduction of our cablegrams, is a great religious romance. He was poor as poverty. While he was puzzling out the details of his invention he was often compelled by sheer necessity to pass twenty-four hours without a meal. The suggestion of a submarine cable emanated largely from his homesickness. He was in Europe; his parents were in America; it took a month to send a letter. A sentence that he had once memorized at Yale haunted him night and day. It was: '*If the circuit of electricity be interrupted, the fluid will become visible; and, when it passes, it will leave an impression upon any intermediate body.*'

'If the circuit be interrupted! If the circuit be interrupted!'
The words took complete possession of his brain. Morse
found it impossible to resist the conclusion that if the interruption of the current must issue in visibility, it ought to
be easy to turn the visibility into a code of signals. The
visibility that resulted from the interruption of the current
would, of course, take the form of a spark. 'Why not make
that spark represent a part of speech, a letter, a number?
Why not make the absence of the spark a part of speech; the
duration of the absence a part? In short, why not have an
alphabet, which should be the voice of electricity?' The idea
reached its climax in his brain on a certain moonlight night
on board the *Sully* as he was returning to America. He paced
the deck all night, and by dawn the alphabet was complete.
In his *History of the Telegraph in America,* Mr. Reid pays an
eloquent tribute to the simplicity and perfection of that
alphabet. 'Men can wink it with their eyes,' he says, 'they
can beat it with their feet, and dying men have used it when
vocal organs and the strength to write were exhausted. The
prisoner can tap it on the wall or grating of his dungeon.
Lovers in distant rooms can converse by it on the gas-pipe.
Its uses are endless. It is the telegraphic language of the
world.' The tremendous and heroic struggle that eventually induced Parliaments and Congresses—always timid of
sensational innovations—to finance Morse's project con-
stitutes one of the great romances of commercial history.
But it is pleasant today to remember that, after patiently
enduring the withering scorn and pitiless ridicule that were
everywhere heaped upon his startling idea of sending words
along wires, he lived to see his invention become the most
amazing financial triumph of his time. Moreover, he lived

to wear the honors and decorations that all the Courts of Europe so plentifully thrust upon him. And all because he was the first to discover the value of an interruption!

How often it happens that a thing only becomes the more impressive and the more effective by being interrupted! Some of the loveliest things in life issue from our interruptions. Indeed, we begin life with an interruption. A woman finds that she must cancel all her engagements; and for awhile we see her face no more. Then she reappears, with a baby in her arms. They say that some women evade marriage and motherhood just because it would involve life in such troublesome interruptions. It is difficult to believe that women can be so blind. The women whose lives have been interrupted in this way have discovered what Samuel Morse discovered fifty years ago, that an interruption may be the most fruitful and vital thing in history.

An interruption, like a rhetorical pause, emphasizes a thing. I recall several utterances that I must have forgotten long ago but for the fact that they were interrupted. Let me mention three. I remember being present, many years ago, at a great prayer meeting in London. A little old gentleman in the body of the hall rose to lead us to the Throne of Grace. His voice was clear as a bell; his diction was reverent and beautiful; he prayed like a man inspired. But all at once his voice became tremulous with emotion, and a moment later it failed him altogether. For a few seconds there was an intense and painful stillness. Then the old gentleman strove bravely to resume his supplication. But after struggling with himself for a second or two, he shook his head sorrowfully. 'Take the meaning, Lord!' he managed to say, 'take the meaning!' and sat down. I am sure I should have forgotten the meeting, the graceful petitions, and the gentle pleader but for the affecting interruption. The interruption lifted it out of the commonplace and lent it a distinction.

The other evening I was conducting a very special Communion Service. To me the occasion was full of sacred significance, for it marked the anniversary of my ordination. An old minister was present, whose long record of distinguished service lent to his gray hairs an added glory. I had asked him to deliver a short pre-communion address. He spoke with evident delight, of the exquisite completeness of his Lord's redemption; and, having poured out his heart to us, he took a step backward as though to resume his seat. But an afterthought seized him; he retraced that single step; and once more took his place at the desk. 'For sixty years,' he said, with manifest emotion, 'for sixty years I have served this Savior, and do you think I have regretted it? Never once!' He resumed his seat, and I announced the next hymn, 'Rock of ages cleft for me'; and even as we sang

> While I draw this fleeting breath,
> When my eyelids close in death,
> When I soar to realms unknown,
> See Thee on Thy judgement throne,
> Rock of Ages, cleft for me,
> Let me hide myself in Thee!

He who had a moment before spoken of the glories of redemption passed serenely into the presence of his Redeemer. Each went his several way, leaving the bread and wine untasted. The service from which we had expected so much had been strangely interrupted. And yet all those who were present felt that it had a beauty, a sacredness, a solemnity, of its own. But for the interruption how soon that gathering would have been forgotten! Now it lives in our memories for ever! We felt as Elisha must have felt when Elijah ascended in a whirlwind before his eyes. The service was perfectly complete, after all.

For the third of these experiences I go back to my Mosgiel days. I remember being asked to speak at a farewell-meeting. The retiring minister had held the charge for over fifty years. When his turn came to speak, he made three desperate efforts to master his emotion. But it was no good. After a few broken sentences he each time collapsed; and his people felt that his silence was more eloquent than his speech could possibly have been. The best things we ever say are the things we never say.

Are there not two such occasions in the Bible—one in each Testament? 'And Moses returned unto the Lord, and said, "Oh, this people have sinned a great sin, and have made them gods of gold. Yet now, if Thou wilt forgive their sin"—' If—what? We shall never know what was in the old leader's mind. The prayer was interrupted; but it is all the finer for being interrupted. There are moments in which the soul leaves speech behind, as a bird leaves the bough, as a butterfly leaves its chrysalis. The New Testament instance is, of course, the story of the prodigal. 'I will arise,' he said, 'and go to my father, and will say unto him, Father, I have sinned against heaven, and before thee, and am no more worthy to be called thy son: make me as one of thy hired servants. And he arose, and came to his father'; but the carefully prepared speech was interrupted. The last clause was never uttered. 'I am no more worthy,' he cried, 'to be called thy son—' That was all; he said nothing about being a hired servant. The revelation of the father's love laughs out of court such squalid stipulations.

Ian Maclaren has put the same story in another setting. Flora Campbell was a daughter, and she came home. 'When she reached the door, her strength had departed and she was not able to knock. She could hear her father feeling for the latch, which for once could not be found, and saying nothing but "Flora, Flora." She had made up some kind of speech, but the only word she ever said was "Father," for Lachlan, who had never even kissed her all the days of her youth, clasped her in his arms and sobbed out blessings over her head.' Flora told Marget Howe afterwards that in the Gaelic there are fifty words for 'darling,' and that her father called her by every one of them the night she came home. And thus her carefully prepared speech was interrupted, and, like the speech of the prodigal, was immeasurably improved by the interruption.

One of the best books in the language was born of an interruption. 'I was just going to say,' it begins, 'when I was interrupted—' The interruption referred to in that opening sentence was, Dr. Oliver Wendell Holmes tells us in the introduction, just a quarter of a century in duration. But if the interruption had never occurred, and if the book had been written when it was first commenced, it is certain that *The Autocrat of the Breakfast-table* would not have been the book that we all treasure so highly and love so well.

But, like language and like literature, life itself gets sometimes interrupted, and generally comes out all the better for the interruption. Who that knows the history of Japan can ever forget the story of the Hon. Alpheus Hardy? Let him tell it in his own words. He says: 'I am not a college man, and it was the bitter disappointment of my life that I could not be one. I wanted to go to college and become a minister; so I went to Phillips Academy to prepare. My health broke down, and, in spite of my determined hope of being able to go on, at last the truth was forced on me that I could not. To tell my disappointment is impossible. It seemed as if all my hope and purpose in life were defeated. "I cannot be God's minister," was the sentence that kept rolling through my mind. When that fact at last became certain to me, one morning alone in my room, my distress was so great that I threw myself flat on the floor. The voiceless cry of my soul was, "O God, I cannot be Thy minister!" Then there came to me as I lay a vision, a new hope, a perception that I could serve God in business with the same devotion as in preaching, and that to make money for God might be my sacred calling. The vision of this service, and its nature as a sacred ministry, were so clear and joyous that I rose to my feet, and, with new hope in my heart, exclaimed aloud, "O God I *can* be Thy minister! I will go back to Boston. I will make money for God, and *that* shall be my ministry!" From that time; I have felt myself as much appointed and ordained to make money for God as if I had been permitted to carry out my own plan and been ordained to preach the gospel. I am God's man, and the ministry to which God has called me is to make and administer money for Him.' He felt that his life had been interrupted, but he determined to make the interruption like the pause in the music that adds effectiveness to all that goes before it and impressiveness to all that follows after.

We all know the sequel. Alpheus Hardy came in course of time to own a line of steamers that traded with Japan.

On one of them a little Japanese boy stowed away, and the captain brought him to Mr. Hardy. Mr. Hardy prayed with him, pointed him to the Savior, and gave him a first-class University education. Then young Neesima went back to Japan to spread the Christian faith from one end of that great empire to the other, and no name in the annals of Japan is more honored than is his. Had Alpheus Hardy had his heart's desire and been a minister, it is exceedingly problematical as to whether he could ever have wrought so fine a work as that. The interruption, like the pause of the orchestra, intensified the beauty of life's harmony.

And, coming back to the unfinished Communion Service, what is death itself but an interruption? Is it not at least conceivable that the first words that most of us will utter on the other shore will be those with which Dr. Oliver Wendell Holmes begins his book? 'I was just going to say, *when I was interrupted*—' Life, like the parts of a serial story, is always '*to be continued.*' At the close of his great history of Peter the Great, Waliszewski comments on the appropriateness of the statuary that adorns the great Czar's tomb. 'At the foot of the mausoleum,' he says, 'an ingenious inspiration has set the symbolic image of a sculptor, beside the unfinished figure his tool has chiseled in the marble.' The work was interrupted. But it is only an interruption. 'I feel,' wrote Victor Hugo, 'I feel that I have not said a thousandth part of what is in me. When I go down to the grave I shall have ended my day's work. But another day will begin next morning. Life closes in the twilight; it opens with the dawn.' As we sometimes sing:

> We'll catch the broken threads again,
> And finish what we here began;

Heaven will the mysteries explain,
And then, sometime, we'll understand.

And, depend upon it, when we resume our old relationships, and take up our tasks anew, we shall find that those fond friendships will have been sweetened, and those hallowed activities perfected, by the temporary break. Life as a whole will have been immeasurably enriched by the interruption.

F. W. Boreham, "Our Interruptions," *The Silver Shadow* (London: Charles H. Kelly, 1918), 243-253.

"PLEASE SHUT THIS GATE!"

It was at Criccieth; and Mr. Lloyd George was playing golf. It happened that, after a round, he and a friend had to cross some fields in which cattle were grazing. 'I was so eager to catch every word that fell from Mr. Lloyd George's lips,' explains his companion, 'that I failed to close one of the gates through which we passed.' But Mr. Lloyd George noticed it, paused, went back and carefully shut and latched the gate. They resumed their walk. 'Do you remember old Dr._____ of _____?' asked Mr. Lloyd George, mentioning a local worthy not long deceased. 'When he was on his death-bed a clergyman went to him and asked him if there was anything he would like to say or any message he wanted to deliver. "No," answered the doctor, "except that through life I think I have always closed the gates behind me!"'

There is, I fancy, a good deal in that. I had in my congregation at Mosgiel a little old man of singular serenity of countenance and sweetness of disposition. Nothing seemed to ruffle his faith or disturb the perfect tranquillity of his spirit. One evening, in the early autumn, he came down to the manse to bring me a basket of freshly gathered fruit. We sat for a while on the verandah chatting. It was an hour for confidences, and he opened his heart to me. I asked him how he accounted for the calm that seemed a perpetual rebuke to our fretfulness and worry. He would not at first admit that he possessed any features that distinguished him from the rest of us. But I pressed my point, and at length he became more communicative.

'Well, I'll tell you this,' he observed, 'I've always made it a rule that, *when I've shut the door, I've shut the door.*'

I sat pondering in silence this cryptic utterance. My friend saw that I was somewhat mystified, and hastened to the rescue.

'Years ago,' he explained, 'I used to take all my troubles to bed with me. I would lie there in the darkness with closed eyes, fretting and worrying all the time. I tossed and turned from one side of the bed to the other, as wide awake as at broad noon. As life went on, the habit grew upon me until it threatened to undermine my health. Then, one night, things reached a crisis. I could not sleep, so I rose from my bed and sat at the open window. The garden below and the fields beyond were flooded in silvery moonlight. Not a breath of wind was stirring; the intense stillness was positively uncanny. The perfect tranquillity mocked the surging tumult of my brain. How quiet the room seemed! And I had entered into it—for what? My behavior seemed absurd in the extreme. I had come to this haven of peace; Nature had wrapped around me her infinite calm; and here was I allowing all the worries of the world to fever my brain and break upon my rest! Why had I locked the office door so carefully if I wished all the ledgers and day-books and order-forms to follow me home? Why had I closed the bedroom door so carefully if I wished all the cares of life to follow me in? I knelt down there at the windowsill, with the delicious air of the still night caressing my face, and I then and there asked God to forgive me. And, since then, *when I've shut a door, I've shut a door!*'

I have often since, when the fret and fever of life have been too much for me, recalled my old friend's story. It is a great thing to be able to go through life, like Mr. Lloyd George's doctor, closing all the gates behind one. Take our decisions, for example. I have sometimes to make up my mind—to buy or to refuse; to sell or to hold; to go or to stay; to accept or to decline. The process of decision should be as leisurely and unhurried as the circumstances will permit. But when a verdict is reached, that judgment should be final. I have no right to insult my own intelligence. I must learn to treat it with respect. There can be no profit in establishing within my mind Courts of Appeal that have no power to carry their findings into effect. Nine times out of ten the verdict of the first court is irrevocable; why then rehear the case? When a man has once made up his mind, let him close the gate behind him, or he will never know happiness again. He has weighed all the evidence; he has balanced all the issues; and he has pronounced sentence. Very well; let it go at that. Why review it again and again? If the decision was sound, why question it? If the decision was doubtful, the sooner it is forgotten the better. Why torture yourself dwelling upon it? The horse is sold; the house is bought; the contract is signed; the situation is declined; the step taken cannot be retraced. A wise man will firmly and finally shut the gate. It is the better way.

I know that it would have been a great thing for my friend George Cairncross if he had been able to acquire this art. George is a minister; we were in college together; and we have been on the most intimate terms ever since. When he entered the ministry, he settled in a small country church at Langford. The work prospered exceedingly, and he was as happy as any man could be. After seven years the pastorate of the church at Grenville, a large town some distance away, fell vacant, and George was unanimously invited. He was at his wits' ends. The cause at Langford was so prosperous and he was so perfectly content. And yet he was young, and Grenville offered much wider scope! But at last the hold of his own people upon his affections proved too strong to be broken; and he declined the tempting overture from the larger church. So far, so good! But it was afterwards that George made his mistake. From that time forth, whenever the least thing went wrong at Langford, George turned his thoughts towards his lost opportunity at Grenville. As surely as a fit of the blues overtook him, he began to dream about Grenville. In poor George's brain Grenville became enveloped in a golden haze of romance. If only he had gone to Grenville! Oh, if only he had accepted the call to Grenville! In his better, wiser, saner, stronger moments he laughed at this frailty of his. He knew that he had decided rightly in remaining at Langford. But there were weaker moments. And in those weaker moments George harked back upon himself. It would have saved him a world of misery if he could have closed firmly and forever the gate that divided the Langford field from the Grenville field.

Eight years later, after a most notable and memorable ministry, George did leave Langford. The church at Bellhaven called him; and, after another desperate inner struggle, he resolved to go. But after the excitement of the farewell, of the removal, and of the welcome, there came the inevitable reaction. Every day George missed at Bellhaven something to which he had grown accustomed at Langford. To be sure, there were compensations; but George was not in the humor to pay much attention to them. The strange conditions grated upon him. At Langford everybody knew him; at Bellhaven he walked the streets a stranger. Every mail from Langford intensified his malady. He thought of the people there who needed him, and whom he seemed to have forsaken; and his soul was filled with bitterness unspeakable. This, so far; as it went, was entirely to his credit; but unfortunately he allowed it to go too far. He let it develop into a habit. Whenever the least thing went wrong at Bellhaven, he convinced himself that he should never have left Langford. It was Langford that now became enveloped in a golden haze. If only he had remained at Langford! Oh, if he had never left Langford! In his better, wiser, saner, stronger moments he felt ashamed of this weakness of his. But there it was! And it would have saved him a world of distress if, when he left the Langford field for the field of Bellhaven, he had closed the gate firmly and finally behind him.

We are expressly told that cattle were grazing in the field that Mr. Lloyd George and his friend were leaving behind them. That is the trouble. There are always things in the fields behind us that may escape unless we carefully close the gates. Who is it that says:

I have closed the door on Fear,
He has lived with me far too long,
If he were to break forth and reappear,
I should lift my eyes and look at the sky,
And sing aloud, and run lightly by:
He will never follow a song.

I have closed the door on Gloom,
His house has too narrow a view,
I must seek for my soul a wider room,
With windows to open and let in the sun,
And radiant lamps when the day is done,
And the breeze of the world blowing through.

It is true that my life cannot be divided into watertight compartments. It is a whole—one and indivisible. But it is a whole, as a fine estate is a whole, with green hedges and white gates conveniently separating one part from another. The gates may be opened and closed at will; but it is good to have them there. We do not want the cattle to stray indiscriminately everywhere. It is pleasant to have some fields from which they are shut out—fields where the children can gather mushrooms and blackberries without fear.

I am very fond of Izaak Walton's *Compleat Angler*. Does the world contain such a triumph of gate-shutting? Our gentle angler lived through the most turbulent years of British history. He was born in the spacious days of great Elizabeth. He was ten years old when the illustrious Queen died. He saw the rise of the Stuarts, the Civil War, the ascendancy of the Puritans, and the execution of Charles the First. He lived all through the days of the Commonwealth; and he witnessed the Restoration! Yet who that has read his book would suspect that bloodshed and civil strife were raging around as he wrote? From the first page to the last, as Professor Jackson has pointed out, we have nothing but 'the murmur of brooks, the rustle of the wind in the trees, the shower falling softly on the teeming earth, the sweet smell of the soil after rain, the shining of the sun on green spaces.' It is a fine thing for a man to be able to shut out the cattle as effectively as that!

Or what about Wordsworth? Was it by some whimsical freak of circumstance that Wellington and Wordsworth were contemporaneous? Was it a mere oddity of chance that a generation almost wholly absorbed in the momentous issues that hung upon the fleets that grappled at Trafalgar, and the armies that fought at Waterloo, should find something very much to its taste in the poetry of Wordsworth? The terrible and long-drawn-out conflict, which ended in the complete overthrow of Napoleon at Waterloo, lasted, with scarcely a break, from 1793 to 1815. Now, singularly enough, it was in the first year of the war—in 1793 that Wordsworth published his first poem; through all these critical years in which the fate of the Empire hung trembling in the balance the poet continued to ravish the ear of the British people; and it was just as the armies of Wellington and Napoleon, of Ney and Blücher, were being drawn up in readiness for 'that world-earthquake, Waterloo,' that the 'Excursion' was given to the nation. While Europe reverberated with the thunder of guns, and shuddered beneath the tramp of armies, Wordsworth sang of the cuckoo and the skylark; of the redbreast and the butterfly; of the linnet and the nightingale; of the sparrow and the daisy. And to such music all the world listened. And why?

Simply because we love to escape at times from the horned cattle, and to roam at will in the meadows in which the cowslip may turn its face to the sun, in which the lark may build her nest among the grasses, and in which lovers may wander in the gloaming undisturbed. Walton and Wordsworth helped people to shut the gate; that was all.

I am writing on the last night of the year. It is an hour for gate-shutting. If the fields behind us contain any creatures that we do not wish to meet again, let us carefully close the gate.

> Let us forget the things that vexed and tried us,
> The worrying things that caused our souls to fret,
> The hopes that, cherished long, were still denied us,
> Let us forget!
> Let us forget the little slights that pained us,
> The greater wrongs that rankle sometimes yet;
> The pride with which some lofty one disdained us,
> Let us forget!

It is of small use hoping for a happy New Year unless I carefully fasten all these gates behind me.

But the best possible illustration of my theme is to be found in the Old Testament. When the children of Israel, in hot haste, escaped from bondage, the Egyptians close upon their heels, a strange thing happened. 'The angel of God, which went before the camp of Israel, removed and went behind them; and the pillar of the cloud went from before their face and stood behind them; and it came between the camp of the Egyptians and the camp of Israel.' A screen of Deity interposed itself between pursued and pursuers. The gate was divinely closed behind them lest the cattle of the land of Egypt should rush out and trample on the chosen people. And, long centuries later, when Israel escaped from Babylon, and dreaded a similar attack from behind, the voice divine again reassured them. 'I, the Lord thy God, will be *thy rearguard.*' There are thousands of things behind me of which I have good reason to be afraid; but it is the glory of the Christian evangel that all the gates may be closed. It is grand to be able to walk in green pastures and beside still waters unafraid of anything that I have left in the perilous fields behind me.

A while ago I preached upon this theme. An old gentleman, a regular member of my congregation, was present. I noticed that he followed me with the closest interest and attention. Next day he quite suddenly passed away. But, before going, he turned to those about him and exclaimed, 'I have shut the gate! I have shut the gate!' Like that of Mr. Lloyd George's doctor, it was a fine testimony! May my sunset be as serene!

F. W. Boreham, "Please Shut the Gate," *The Silver Shadow* (London: The Epworth Press, 1918), 109-119.

THE HOUSE THAT JACK BUILT

No man can do one thing without doing a million things.
That is the moral of *The House that Jack Built.* I am coming
to a theory of my own concerning nursery rhymes. We have
always supposed them to be silly little sayings composed by
simpletons to tickle the ears of small children. It is open
to question. Mr. G. K. Chesterton has evolved a world of
philosophy out of *Jack the Giant Killer.* Mrs. Barclay, in
The Rosary, has made skillful use of *Little Jack Horner.* And
it has been suggested that the tragedy of *Humpty Dumpty*
was originally penned to demonstrate to hesitating politi-
cians the extreme peril of sitting on a fence. However that
may be, the intricate comedy of *The House That Jack Built*
is indisputable philosophy. I shall not be astonished if some
learned antiquarian proves to us that these enchanting
fables were penned by the seven wise men of Greece, who,
despairing of instilling their subtle but priceless conclusions
into the minds of their contemporaries, embalmed them,
like bees in amber, in these charming little romances, and

thus gave them immortality, fondly hoping that, in some remote period of world-history, a generation would arise that would possess the intellectual acumen and spiritual discernment that would enable it to recognize and disinter the hoarded philosophic treasure.

Now, in the story of *The House that Jack Built,* the authors were clearly grappling with the profound mystery of Influence. Jack, probably with an eye on some blushing Jill, builds a house, and see what a train of consequences follows, each promoted and influenced by the other! This is the splendid problem of every generation. On every hand people are inquiring with feverish anxiety as to the precise influence of mind upon matter; of mind upon mind; and of the invisible upon the material. The master minds of the age are absorbed in the attempt to read aright this fascinating but elusive riddle. As the pursuit has proceeded, it has become clear that, as a matter of fact, every object has its own attracting or repelling influence on every other object. And, whether we like it or not, every life has its own distinct and formative influence on every other life. It is not that we *may* wield an influence; the eternal laws do not hinge on haps and chances; it is that we *must* and *do* exert that influence. It is the quality and direction in which the force shall be spent that alone remains for our own determination.

I

The story of *The House that Jack Built* enshrines the notable fact that these radiations of energy may be said to work along three definite lines.

First of all, there is the *cumulative* line of influence. The house is built. Now see what happens. Malt is introduced, then a rat, then a cat, then a dog; then a cow; and so on. Each is larger than the other; the thing gathers momentum as it evolves and proceeds. All of which is wonderfully true to life. I need scarcely mention Professor Tate's well-known demonstration with the iron cylinder. The Professor would suspend the cylinder by a cord in his classroom and then invite his students to pelt it with paper pellets. For a while the pellets would produce no visible effect, but gradually a thrill would become perceptible; then a movement; and at last the whole cylinder would swing to and fro. The cumulative influence of many concussions achieved the desired end. The same thing happened when Sir Christopher Wren was pulling down Old St. Paul's, prior to the erection of the present stately fabric. He employed a battering-ram on the stubborn structure; and, as many blows fell with no apparent effect upon the massive walls, he encouraged the men by exclaiming: 'Every blow tells!' And at last one blow, no heavier than the rest, reduced the splendid pile to ruins. The application of this truth to moral and religious effort is obvious. 'Every blow tells!' There is the cumulative line of influence to be reckoned with.

II

Then there is, in this pretty ballad, what may be classified as the *simple* or *direct* line of influence. It is all so natural and so easy to trace. What more natural than that Jack should build a house? Every Jack should. And having built it, what more natural than that he should store it? And what more natural than that the stores should attract a rat, and the rat a cat, and the cat a dog, and so on. These perpetuations of cause and effect, when traced from first to last, amaze us by their very simplicity, which also is absolutely scientific. Let me give one or two illustrations. We are all familiar with the colossal proportions of the banana traffic of the Pacific Islands. In his *Forty Years' Mission Work,* the Rev. A. W. Murray, the pioneer missionary, points out that this stupendous trade sprang from a single bunch of bananas which the Duke of Devonshire presented to the heroic John Williams when he came out as the ambassador of Jesus Christ to the South Sea Islands!

This simple or direct line of influence governs the bane as well as the boon. Darwin tells us, in his *Voyage of the Beagle,* that the dock-weeds of these southern climes are a perpetual memorial to the rascality of an English sailor who sold the seed as tobacco-seed to the Maoris before the tides of immigration set in. And so the law asserts itself. I set in motion a tide of influence, and it goes on spreading and growing long after I have lost all trace of it—long after I myself am dead and forgotten.

One of the most striking illustrations of the operation of this line of influence on a spiritual plane is provided by the record of Richard Sibbes, the Puritan. Richard Sibbes wrote *The Bruised Reed* and wondered if it was worth while. But afterwards *The Bruised Reed* was the means of the conversion of the saintly Richard Baxter of Kidderminster, and Baxter wrote his epochmaking *Call to the Unconverted.* Then Baxter's *Call* lit the fire in the heart of Philip Doddridge, which produced *The Rise and Progress of Religion in the Soul.* And that book, having fallen into the hands of William Wilberforce and changed his life, led Wilberforce to write *The Practical View of Christianity.* Then Leigh Richmond was converted by reading Wilberforce's book, and in his turn wrote *The Dairyman's Daughter. The Dairyman's Daughter,* besides being the most powerful religious influence in the early life of Queen Victoria, had a good deal to do with the transformation of Thomas Chalmers, and, through him, touched the whole wide world.

III

But it is time that we noticed that our story illustrates a third and still more bewildering line of influence—the *indirect* or *complex* line of influence. The tale opens, it will be noticed, in the realm of domestic economy. Jack builds a house and stores it. That is perfectly simple. But the immediate consequences affect the world of zoology and natural history. Rats, dogs, cats, cows are all acted upon by Jack's enterprise. And then the more remote consequences penetrate the fields of romance and religion. There is a maiden all forlorn, a man all tattered and torn, and a priest all shaven and shorn. Who would have dreamed, when Jack laid the foundations of his future dwelling, that he was casting his magic spell over the destinies of these invisible actors? It is very interesting, very wonderful, and still very true to the stern facts of life. In his *Origin of Species,* Darwin shows that, at one time, the cultivation of red clover depended upon the cultivation of cats! The clover could then only be fertilized by humble bees. The nests of the humble bees were destroyed by field-mice. The farmer, therefore, who wished his clover to flourish, cultivated an alliance with the cats in order that, the mice being destroyed, the bees might multiply, and the clover in consequence luxuriate. That is influence working along an indirect or complex line. Or look at another instance. Sir Charles Lyell argues that the amount of song in the great forests of Central America depends upon the quantity of seal-fishing in the North Atlantic during the preceding season. For, if the seal-fishing is neglected, seals abound in consequence; if seals abound, the salmon are devoured. But, along the banks of the great American rivers, the otters are waiting for the coming of the salmon; and if, through the decay of sealing, the salmon do not come up stream, the otters turn inland and destroy the young birds!

It would be easy to demonstrate, by a score of examples, the operation of this intricate law in everyday life. There is, for example, the story of the Haldanes. In his earlier days, James Haldane commanded a man-of-war, the *Melville Castle*. One day, in the heat of an action, he ordered up a fresh set of men to take the places of those who had been killed by a broadside of the enemy. The men, seeing the mangled bodies of their comrades, instinctively recoiled and shrank back. James Haldane poured forth a volley of oaths, and included a terrible and blasphemous prayer. A Christian seaman, whose name nobody knows, went straight up to his captain and respectfully but fearlessly asked him how he would like his awful prayer to be literally answered. The captain was smitten through and through. From that day he was a changed man. He lived for fifty-four years to preach the gospel. His own brother, Robert, whom all the world knows as an able and learned commentator, was one of the first-fruits of his ministry.

Robert, in his turn, went to Geneva, and, while there, was the means of the conversion of a band of young men which included Felix Neff, the enthusiastic evangelist of the High Alps; Merle Daubigne, the historian of the Reformation; and Frederick Monod, one of the pillars of the Evangelical Church in France. And so the action of a quiet able-bodied seaman in rebuking his captain's blasphemy, by an indirect but distinctly traceable line of influence, shook all Europe and still moves the world.

Now the whole point of the story is that, in the eternal scheme of things of which we form a part, there is no waste of energy. Only once in ten thousand times can one trace the line along which the influence of his action or his work may move. But whether he can trace it or not, it moves, and moves grandly and resistlessly to its goal. That is one of the eternal laws on which the universe is built. That thought adds a new dignity, a new solemnity, a new hope, and a new fear to every moment of one's life.

> You cannot raise the dead, nor from the soil
> Glean precious dust. But you can live
> A life that tells on other lives, and makes
> The world less full of evil and of pain,
> A life which, like a pebble dropped in the sea,
> Sends its wide circles to a hundred shores.

Whatever Influence is, all thinkers are agreed that every ounce of force holds possibilities of infinite application and reverberation. Each life has its own peculiar and unsuspected radiations, which, directly or remotely, affect every other life. It is all very wonderful and very terrible and very beautiful. It helps me to believe all that the Scriptures have

said about no seed being sown in vain and about no cup of
cold water losing its reward. And it helps me to understand
what Longfellow meant when he said:—

> I shot an arrow into the air,
> It fell to earth, I knew not where;
> For, so swiftly it flew, the sight
> Could not follow it in its flight.

> I breathed a song into the air,
> It fell to earth, I knew not where;
> For who has sight so keen and strong,
> That it can follow the flight of song?

> Long, long afterward, in an oak,
> I found the arrow, still unbroken;
> And the song, from beginning to end,
> I found again in the heart of a friend.

The radiations and reactions and repercussions and.
reverberations of life are simply infinite. To explore them is
to explore infinity; to comprehend them is to comprehend
eternity. We are living in a world in which no person can do
one thing without doing a million things.

F. W. Boreham, "The House that Jack Built," *The Drums of
Dawn* (London: The Epworth Press, 1933, 254-262.

THE EYES OF EASTER

On Good Friday we turn to Calvary with Easter eyes. Bunyan tells us how it is done. When Christian came to the Cross and was welcomed by the Three Shining Ones, 'he looked—and looked—and looked again!' Three looks; but three different looks! The first was the Look *Positive;* the second was the Look *Comparative;* the third was the Look *Superlative.*

I

The Churches of the world have been celebrating the centenary of the conversion of C. H. Spurgeon. It was a snowy Sunday in the middle of last century. As the caretaker fought his way through the storm from his cottage to the chapel in Artillery Street, Colchester (which, to my delight, I myself had the privilege of visiting a few years back), he wondered whether, on such a wild and wintry day, anyone would venture out. He unbolted the chapel doors and lit the furnace under the stove.

Half an hour later the preacher glanced nervously round upon three hundred empty seats. Nearly empty, but not quite, for there were a dozen or fifteen of the regular worshippers present, and there was a boy sitting under the gallery who, intending to worship at a distant sanctuary, had been driven by the storm to shelter in this one.

People who had braved such a morning deserved all the help that could be given them, and the strange boy under the gallery ought not to be sent back into the storm feeling that there was nothing in the service for him. And so the preacher determined to make the most of his opportunity, and he did.

The boy under the gallery! A marble tablet now adorns the wall near the seat which he occupied that snowy day. The inscription records that, that very morning, the boy sitting under the gallery was converted! He was only fifteen, and he died at fifty-seven. But, in the course of the intervening years, he preached the gospel to millions and led thousands upon thousands into the kingdom and service of Jesus Christ.

It has often been said that, as with the leaves of the forest, no two conversions are alike: each has its own distinctive features. Yet, as with the leaves of the forest, all conversions answer to a general pattern. However dissimilar the externals, in essence they are very similar.

II

Can history present two conversion stories that stand in more dramatic contrast, the one with the other, and yet that more closely resemble each other, than those of Francis d'Assisi and C. H. Spurgeon?

London was hardly larger than a modern village in the time of Francis d'Assisi and wild boars roamed in the forests that then covered the sites of our great modern cities. While King John was signing the Magna Carta, Francis was at Rome seeking recognition for his brotherhood of friars. It was the age of the Crusaders and the Troubadours. Yet, as I read the moving record of his great spiritual experience, I forget that I have invaded a period in which English history was only beginning to unfold.

The lithe and graceful figure of Francis, with his dark, eloquent, but sparkling eyes, his wealthy shock of jet black hair, his soft, rich, sonorous voice and his gay but faultless attire, was the soul and center of every youthful revel. He was, as Sir James Stephen says, foremost in every feat of arms, first in every triumph of scholarship and the gayest figure in every festival. 'The brightest eyes in Assisi, dazzled by so many graces, and the most reverend brows there, acknowledging such early wisdom, were alike bent with admiration towards him.' His bewitching personality, his rollicking gaiety, his brooding thoughtfulness, his dauntless courage and his courtly ways swept all men off their feet; he had but to lead and they instinctively followed; he commanded and they unquestionably obeyed.

And the story of his conversion? Come with me! As, with your face towards Spello, you follow the windings of the Via Francesca, you will find the little church of St. Damian's on the slope of the hill outside the city walls. It is reached by a short walk over a stony path, shaded with olive trees, amid odors of lavender and rosemary. 'Standing on the top of a hillock, the entire plain is visible through a curtain of cypresses and pines which seem to be trying to hide the humble hermitage and set up an ideal barrier between it and the noisy world.' Francis was particularly fond of this wooded walk and of the sanctuary to which it led. In pensive moments, when it was more than usually evident to him that, with all his frolics, he had yet to discover the fountain of true gladness, he turned his face this way.

In this little chapel in the woods, there was a crucifix that held a strange fascination for Francis. The thorn-crowned face was irresistibly beautiful; the sad eyes wonderfully appealing. Francis was one day bowing before this crucifix when, suddenly, everything seemed to fade from before his eyes. The church, the altar, the crucifix itself, all vanished. He was alone with his living and glorified Lord! In that transforming moment, as Canon Adderley says, Christ became the center of his being, the soul of his soul. He looked and looked and looked again; feasting his spirit on the vision of the Savior who had died for his redemption. He vowed that, in all the days to come, he would spend and be spent in His service.

Francis never forgot that moment. His whole soul overflowed with the intensity of his affection for his Savior. To the end of his days he could never think of the Cross without tears.

III

The conversion of Francis was effected six hundred years before the conversion of Mr. Spurgeon. Yet that conversion in the ruined church of St. Damian's in Italy is the very counterpart of that later conversion in the little chapel at Artillery Street, Colchester.

'Look to Jesus!' cried the preacher at Colchester that Sunday morning.

'Look to Jesus! See, He sweats great drops of blood; He hangs upon the Cross; He dies—and dies for you! Look to Jesus, young man, look to Jesus; look and live!'

'I looked,' says Mr. Spurgeon, 'I looked that very moment and was saved!'

'Francis looked to the Crucified,' says his biographer, in narrating the incident that transformed his hero's life. 'It was a look of faith; a look of love; a look that had all his soul in it; a look which did not attempt to investigate but which was content to receive. He looked, and, looking, entered into life.'

You can take the sentences from the *Life of Francis* and transfer them to the *Life of Spurgeon,* or vice versa, and they will fit their new environment with the most perfect historical accuracy.

Now, somewhere midway between the time of Francis and the time of Spurgeon stands the sturdy and satisfying figure of John Bunyan. And, in his *Pilgrim's Progress,* John Bunyan paints a vivid and unforgettable picture that, brushing aside the external trappings of this medieval scene in Italy, and the non-essential drapery of this nineteenth century happening in Essex, unifies and harmonizes and co-ordinates the two striking stories. It is the passage that tells of Christian's arrival at the Cross. Here it is:

Then was Christian glad and lightsome, and said with a merry heart: He hath given me rest by His sorrow and life by His death! Then he stood still for awhile to look and wonder:

for it was very surprising to him that the sight of the Cross should thus ease him of his burden. He looked, therefore, and looked again, even till the springs that were in his head sent the waters down his cheeks. Now as he stood looking and weeping, behold, three Shining Ones came to him and saluted him with 'Peace be to thee.' So the first said to him, 'Thy sins are forgiven'; the second stripped him of his rags and clothed him with change of raiment; the third also set a mark in his forehead and gave him a roll with a seal upon it, which he bade him look on as he ran. So they went their way. Then Christian gave three leaps for joy and went on singing.

'I looked and looked and looked again,' says Bunyan's pilgrim. Three looks; the look that was *good,* the look that was *better* and the look that was *best!* Bunyan himself analyses those three looks.

> '*I looked*'; it was the *Look Positive;* the Look of *Astonishment.*
> '*And looked*'; it was the *Look Comparative;* the Look of *Wonder.*
> '*And looked again!*' It was the *Look Superlative;* the Look of *Faith.*

The *first* look was a look of *Surprise:* 'for it was *very surprising* to him that the sight of the Cross should thus ease him of his burden.' The Cross never finds its rightful place in a man's heart until, as in the experiences of Francis and of Spurgeon, it takes his breath away. It becomes life's supreme and most bewildering astonishment. Love so *amazing!* At his mother's knee a man may have heard again and again the sweet, sad story of the Crucifixion. Hundreds of times its pathos may have been impressed upon him by earnest teachers and eloquent preachers. The first songs that he learned to sing may have fastened upon his heart the pitifulness of the world's great tragedy. By iteration and reiteration, by constant representation in song and picture and speech, the story of the Cross may have become the most familiar story a man has ever heard. It matters nothing. A day will come—the greatest day in his soul's long pilgrimage—in which the Cross will take to itself all the characteristics of an incredible sensation. He will scarcely believe the evidence of his senses. The blood will leave his face; his heart will stop beating and his nerves will quiver with excitement. His whole soul will be thrown into a tumult of agitation. The Cross will suddenly become *very surprising* to him. There is all the difference in the world between being touched to tears by the tender pathos of a thousand love-stories and *falling in love yourself!* The same immeasurable gulf yawns between the emotion with which one hears, as an historic recital, the moving story of the Crucifixion and the emotion with which one suddenly recognizes, as his own personal Redeemer, the Savior who died upon the Cross.

The *second* look was a look of *Wonder.* 'Then he stood for awhile,' Bunyan says, '*to look and wonder.*' Wonder follows naturally upon surprise. So far from their being two names for the same thing, it may be said that wonder cannot come to its own as long as surprise is present. While the faculties are still paralyzed by astonishment, wonder cannot do its best work. Wonder is far greater than surprise. Surprise is sudden and fleeting; it evaporates quickly; the astonishment of yesterday becomes the commonplace of today. But wonder remains; it is abiding and permanent.

When, as a small child, I was first permitted to go outdoors at night, I was astonished to see the stars glittering in the skies above me. When, nowadays, I leave home of an evening, the stars fail to surprise me. But, as I observe their movements, admire their arrangement, and contemplate their multitude and immensity, I am filled with a wonder such as, in infancy, I never knew. When springtime follows on the heels of winter, it does not surprise me; on the contrary, I should be surprised if it did not come. But it fills me with wonder. And when, some day, a springtime comes that stirs within me no such feeling; when I stare vacantly and unwonderingly upon the buds in the hedgerow, the nests in the elms and the lambs in the meadows, it will be a sign of the failure of my powers. I shall cease to *wonder* just before I cease to *live*.

The *third* look is the look of *Faith*. The phraseology that connects *looking* with *believing is* very ancient; and it has lasted so long because it is so true to life and experience. Adopting the symbolism of the serpent in the wilderness, and the Savior's comment on that historic imagery, the hymn says that 'There is life for a look at the Crucified One.' '*Look unto Me and be ye saved!*' cried the preacher at Colchester.

IV

I look to my doctor to heal me when I am hurt; I look to my lawyer to advise me when I am perplexed; I look to my tradesman to bring my daily supplies to my door; and Bunyan's pilgrim discovered that there is One to whom I may look with confidence when my soul aches for deliverance. This is the look *of Faith:* the *Look Superlative*.

Christian's three looks at the Cross were followed by three leaps for joy, and then he went on his way singing. It is ever so. The Cross is the inspiration for our blithest songs. Francis left St. Damian's singing; young Spurgeon left Artillery Street singing; the Savior Himself, for very joy that He could save the world by dying for it, sang as He abandoned Himself to His anguish. And every man who, like Bunyan's pilgrim, has looked and looked and looked again upon the Cross, has found his soul flooded with a sudden melody. 'He went on his way singing'; and, singing as the birds sing in the full-throated ecstasy of a summer's morning, he passes from our sight.

F. W. Boreham, "The Eyes of Easter," *Arrows of Desire* (London: The Epworth Press, 1951), 42-48.

SERMONS AND SANDWICHES

It was the church anniversary. On the Sunday there were special sermons, solemn praise, and stately anthems. Everything was inspiring, impressive, sublime. On the Monday there were sandwiches, cream puffs, and jam-tarts. The steaming urns imparted a genial glow to the spirits of the guests, for waves of laughter rippled and broke through the hum of friendly chatter. I had taken part in the solemn services of the Sunday, and had been asked to speak at the tea-meeting on the Monday. I drew aside to collect my thoughts. But my thoughts politely, but firmly, declined to be collected. They insisted on propounding to me this arresting conundrum—tell us, they clamored, the philosophical connection between the *sermons* of yesterday and the *sandwiches* of today. What relation exists between singing and scones? What fellowship hath religion with revelry? Why follow the sacred worship of the Lord's Day with a carnival of confectionery?

I took my Bible from my pocket, and had not to search far before I came upon a clue. On one of the very earliest pages of the sacred records I lit upon a significant statement. It occurs at a crisis in Hebrew history. It was a time of wealthy revelation and divine illumination. Here it is: 'They saw God, and did eat and drink.' There you have revelation and revelry side by side. There you have the secret of all worship and the germ of all tea-meetings. 'They saw God'—that is the principle of the *sermon;* 'and did eat and drink'—that is the principle of the *sandwich.* What more could I desire? Yet I read on, and, to my amazement, I found these two great principles running side by side, like a pair of white horses perfectly matched, through the entire volume. The sandwich was never far from the sermon.

In the Old Testament all the stirring seasons of spiritual elevation and national enlightenment were *Feasts*—the Feast of Pentecost, the Feast of Tabernacles, the Feast of Passover, the Feast of Trumpets, the Feast of Dedication, and so on. Revelation blends with revelry. The chapter that tells of Israel's redemption from Egypt by the shedding of blood—a classic of revelation—tells also, in precise and graphic detail, of the eating of the lamb. The passage that tells how Elijah saw the angel tells also how the angel said, 'Arise and eat!' 'And, behold, a cake baked on the coals, and a cruse of water.'

The sandwich principle keeps pace with the sermon principle. Revelry goes hand in hand with revelation. The tea-meeting is never far from the special services. But the most revealing element in the ancient economy was its law of sacrifice. The old dispensation crystallized itself in the altar. And here we all sit at the feet of Professor Robertson

Smith. He made this theme peculiarly his own. And he fearlessly affirms that we cannot understand that solemn and striking symbol of patriarchal faith unless we grasp the fact that the altar was first of all a table. 'This,' he says, 'is the key to the whole subject of sacrifice, and the basis of all Semitic covenants. When the two parties have eaten of the same victim, and thus become participants in a common life, a living bond of union is established between them, and they are no longer enemies, but brothers.' Here, then, are the two laws—the law of the sermon and the law of the sandwich, the principle of revelation and the principle of revelry—in closest juxtaposition at the very climax of the old world's illumination.

Crossing the border-line into the New Testament, the same singular conjunction is everywhere. 'This beginning of miracles did Jesus in Cana of Galilee, and manifested forth His glory.' The revelation was a revelry. It was at a marriage feast. Later miracles followed the same line—the feeding of four thousand, the feeding of five thousand, and so on. Loaves and fishes—the representation of the sandwich—were never far from the most revealing sermons of the Son of Man. And even when, after His resurrection, He deigns to show Himself to His astounded fishermen, He feeds them. 'And they saw a fire of coals, and fish laid thereon, and bread.' Revelation and revelry are together still. And just as the Old Testament reaches its natural climax in the Altar of Sacrifice, so the New Testament reaches its culminating revelation in the Table of the Lord. There 'we see God, and do eat and drink.' The two principles join hand in hand. And even when the Great Revealer spoke of heaven, these two thoughts were always in His mind.

Heaven is a place of revelation and of revelry. There the pure in heart see God; and there we sit down at the Marriage Supper of the Lamb. People often do things, as the swallows do, under the guidance of some sure instinct, yet without detecting, or even desiring, any explanation of their odd behavior. It is thus that the Church has wedded her revelries to her revelations. She has rightly set the sandwich over against the sermon. The union is indissoluble. The solemn service and the social meal are inseparable. These two hath God joined together.

Now in these two elements I find my bond of brotherhood with the holiest and the lowliest. Among the angels and archangels and all the company of the heavenly host I know not what seraphic spirits may burn. But I know that there is no altitude higher than this to which they can attain—they see God! But so do I. Then they and I are brothers. In the splendid revelations of Christian worship we stand allied to the holiest in the height.

And in eating and drinking, on the other hand, we are kinned to the lowliest. I watch the birds as they fly. It seems to me that they live in one element, and I in another; we have nothing in common. I watch the rabbit as he shyly peeps from his burrow. How far removed his life from mine! I watch the trout as they flash and dart in the shades and shallows of the stream. There is no point of fellowship between them and me. But wait! The rabbit sits upon his haunches nibbling at a blade of grass, on which a dewdrop glistens. He eats and drinks! So do I. The bird flutters down from the bough to seize a morsel on the lawn. He eats and drinks! So do I. The fish come darting up the stream to devour the gnats that, in trying to escape the birds, have fallen upon the glassy surface. They eat and drink! So do I. If the sermon allies me to angels and to seraphs, the sandwich allies me to all things furry and feathered and finny. When we were prattlers our nurses used to amuse us with fantastic pictures of lions and storks and ants and dolphins and people all sitting down, cheek by jowl, at the same table.

Later on we despised the old print as a furious freak of some farcical fancy. But now we know that it was nothing of the kind. It was a severely accurate delineation of the real and sober truth. Indeed, it was less than the truth, for no superhuman guests were there. The universe is a banqueting-table. That sage old friar—Francis d'Assisi—was within the mark, after all, when he addressed the creatures as Brother Hare, Sister Lark, Brother Wolf, and so on. The *sermon* element brings me into intimate and fraternal relationship with all the flaming hosts above. The *sandwich* element brings me into league with the tigers, and the tomtits, and the trout. The special services of anniversary Sunday, and the tea-meeting of the Monday, set forth in harmonious combination the breadth and catholicity of man's holiest and lowliest brotherhoods.

But the instinct of the tea-meeting tells me yet one other thing. I see now that I have misinterpreted the majesty of God. 'It is the pathetic fate of Deity,' says Pascal, 'to be everlastingly misunderstood.' I had always supposed that the glory of God was embarrassing, bewildering, dazzling! I had thought of it as repelling, terrifying, paralyzing! But now I see that it is nothing of the kind. 'They saw God, and did eat and drink.' Even a cat, will not eat in a strange house, nor a bird in a strange cage. Eating and drinking are symbols of familiarity. We feel at home. We bring our friends to our tables that they may realize their welcome. My ugly thought of God was a caricature, a parody, an insult. Man was made for God, and only finds his perfect poise in His presence. To see God is to eat and drink—to be perfectly, peacefully, reverently, restfully, delightfully at home.

' "I have served God, and feared Him with all my heart," says poor Rufus Webb in Miss Ellen Thorneycroft Fowler's *Fuel of Fire.*

' "That may be, but you have never *loved* nor *trusted* Him!" replied the minister.

'The dying man lay silent for a few minutes, with closed eyes. Then he opened them again, and said, "I wonder if you are right, and I have misjudged Him all these years?"

' "I am sure of it."

' "And do you think He will pardon me that also, in addition to my many other sins?"

' "I am sure of it," repeated the vicar, "although it is hard, even for Him, to be misjudged by those whom He loves; there are few things harder." '

It is even so. I heard the solemn pathos of this philosophy jingled out in the clatter of the cups and the spoons at the tea-meeting. 'A glorious high throne is the place of *our sanctuary.*' It is not repelling; it is restful. He who sees God eats and drinks. The sandwiches naturally follow the sermons. 'If any man hear My voice I will come in to him, and will sup with him, and he with Me.'

F. W. Boreham, "Sermons and Sandwiches," *The Luggage of Life* (London: Charles H. Kelly, 1912), 185-192.

LEAD, KINDLY LIGHT

At two most crucial points Christianity fearlessly challenges experiment, and bravely dares a test. The first is in the matter of *Prayer*. The second is in the matter of *Guidance*. If it can be proved that the great Father ever allows any of His children to cry to Him in vain, or if it can be shown that He leaves any of them to stumble home in the dark as best they can, then Christianity has broken down. It stands exposed and exploded. But can it? There is no cause for alarm. In *The Luggage of Life* I have tried to show that even in our dear earthly homes, however crowded with cots they may become, each child finds a place of his own, and his voice is loved and listened to. The largeness of the family does not diminish the affection for the individual; and earthly parentage is, after all, but a spark from the divine flame. It is inconceivable that the Father of fatherhood will overlook one of His children simply because He has 'so much to see to.' It is our Lord's own tender and beautiful argument: 'If

ye then, being evil … *how much more* shall your heavenly
Father?' Could anything be more satisfying or convincing?
But to come to the second matter. We have all known
the torture of indecision. To buy or not to buy? To accept
or to decline? To go or to stay? To turn this way or that? It is
dreadful! Now, the question is: Are we justified, in our seasons of perplexity, in expecting to hear a guiding voice, or
to discern a shining light, or to see a beckoning hand? Must
we plunge into the gloom, or may we follow the gleam? Is
there a Kindly Light that leads? If we reply in the negative,
a hundred exceeding great and precious promises become
instantly unintelligible, and, in consequence, all Scripture
falls under suspicion of being disingenuous and insincere.
And yet, on the other hand, it is so difficult, in our distraction, to hear that voice, to discern that light, to see that
beckoning hand.

Think of that memorable day in the life of Goethe.
'A delicious sadness subdued his thoughts,' his biographer
tells us, 'as he wandered dreamily along the banks of the
Lahn. The lovely scenes which met his eye solicited his
pencil, awakening once more the ineffectual desire, which
from time to time haunted him, of becoming a painter.
The desire, often suppressed, now rose up in such serious
shape that he resolved to settle for ever whether he should
devote himself to art or not. The test was curious. The river
glided beneath, now flashing in the sunlight, now partially
concealed by willows. Taking a knife from his pocket, he
flung it with his left hand into the river, having previously
resolved that, if he saw it fall, he was to become an artist; but if the sinking knife was concealed by the willows,
he was to abandon the idea. No ancient oracle was ever

more ambiguous than the answer now given him. The willows concealed the sinking knife; but the water splashed up like a fountain, and was distinctly visible. So indefinite an answer left him still in doubt.' It is thus that our wayward will-o'-the-wisps torment us. There must be a more excellent way. There is! I hazard three suggestions.

I

The Kindly Light must be treated *very Patiently*. May I draw upon my memory? Just after I settled in my New Zealand manse it was my great privilege to entertain one of the most gifted, most experienced, and most gracious of our ministers. I felt it to be a priceless opportunity, and I sought his counsel concerning all my early ministerial difficulties. One lovely morning we were sitting together on the verandah, looking away across the golden plains to the purple and sunlit mountains, when I broached to him this very question. 'Can a man be quite sure,' I asked, 'that, in the hour of perplexity, he will be *rightly led*? Can he feel secure against *a false step*?' I shall never forget his reply. He sprang from his deck chair and came earnestly towards me. 'I am certain of it,' he exclaimed, 'if he will but *give God time!* Remember *that* as long as you live,' he added entreatingly—'GIVE GOD TIME!'

More than ten years later I found myself face to face with a crisis. I had to make a decision on which my whole life's work depended, and I had to make the decision by five o'clock—the hour at which the telegraph office closed—on a certain Saturday evening. It chanced once more that a minister was my guest. But he could not help me. He thought it vastly improbable that God could concern Himself about individual trivialities. 'The Lord has so much to see to … such a lot of beds in the ward!' He was inclined to think that a certain element of chance dominated our mortality, that a man was bound to take certain risks, and that life was very much like a lottery. 'And if a man make a mistake at a critical juncture like this?' I asked anxiously. He shrugged his shoulders.

'And after that the dark.' I remember with a shudder how my faith winced and staggered under that blow. But I thought of the sunny morning on the verandah ten years before, and clutched desperately and wildly at my old faith. Saturday came. I positively had not the ghost of a notion as to what I ought to do. At five minutes to five I was at the telegraph office, still in hopeless confusion. At three minutes to five a man rode up on a bicycle. So far as I knew, he was absolutely ignorant of the crisis through which I was floundering. But he told me something that relieved the entire situation, and made my course as clear as noonday, and by five o'clock the message had been dispatched.

Dr. Jowett, of New York, says that he was once in the most pitiful perplexity, and consulted Dr. Berry, of Wolverhampton. 'What would you do if you were in my place?' he entreated. 'I don't know, Jowett, I am not there, and you are not there yet! When have you to act?' 'On Friday,' Dr. Jowett replied. 'Then,' answered Berry, 'you will find your way perfectly clear on Friday! The Lord will not fail you!' And, surely enough, on Friday all was plain.

One of the very greatest and wisest of all Queen Victoria's diplomatists has left it on record that it became an inveterate habit of his mind never to allow any opinion on any subject to crystallize until it became necessary to arrive at a practical decision. Give God time, and even when the knife flashes in air the ram will be seen caught in the thicket! Give God time, and even when Pharaoh's host is on Israel's heels a path through the waters will suddenly open! Give God time, and when the bed of the brook is dry Elijah shall hear the guiding voice! Yes, the Kindly Light must be treated very patiently.

II

And very obediently! This has never been better put than in *Robinson Crusoe*, the story of whose experiences is one of the finest religious classics in our literature. We all recall the agony of consternation into which he was thrown on discovering that he was not alone on his island. The presence of savages changed the outlook completely, and he knew not which way to turn. In his confusion he sought the divine guidance, and in language that has never been excelled by Quaker or by mystic he tells at length of those secret hints given to his spirit, directing him, in opposition to his inclinations, to go this way or that way, by means of which his life was preserved from a thousand perils. To his instant and unquestioning response to these 'secret hints and pressings of mind' he attributed everything. The whole passage is worthy of a careful reperusal. It is a gem.

From Robinson Crusoe to Paul is not so far a cry as it seems. There is nothing in the New Testament more dramatic than the great missionary's silent journey across Asia. He set his face towards the evangelization of the stately commercial capitals of the Eastern world. But in each place

he was 'forbidden of the Holy Ghost to preach the Word,'
and trudged on in stillness. 'The Spirit suffered him not.'
As the Quakers would say, 'there was a stop in his mind
against it.'

> I hear a voice you cannot hear,
> Which says I must not stay;
> I see a hand you cannot see,
> Which beckons me away.

And the result of Paul's implicit obedience to that
mysterious inward restraint was—EUROPE! It shifted
the balance of power, and altered the face of the world.
As Benjamin Kidd has demonstrated, the great western
empires sprang out of that extraordinary silence, that mys-
tical submission. It is ever so. Carey planned to evangelize
the South Seas. The inward monitor said *India!* Livingstone selected China. The voice said *Africa!* And who that
realizes what Europe has meant to the world, what Carey
has meant to India, and what Livingstone has meant to
Africa, shall doubt the wisdom of unquestioning compli-
ance with that secret dictate? Yes, the Kindly Light must
be treated very obediently.

III

And very gratefully! For, however difficult it may be to see
the gleam leading on through the gloom, it is never difficult, on looking back, to see that we have been led. A brilliant essayist has said that 'John Wesley was being trained
for his mission long before he appeared on this planet. The
High Churchmanship of his father, the Puritan strain in his

wonderful mother—were not these master-elements in the forming of his soul?' So early the Kindly Light was leading! With almost wearisome monotony biographers point out to us the wonderful way in which each separate phase of life peculiarly fits a person for the next. To take a single illustration, which is typical of scores, and which I select only because of its conciseness, Sir Alfred Lyall, in his *Life of Lord Dufferin,* remarks: 'The appointments which he had previously held had been of such a kind that if they had been purposely undertaken as a course of preparatory training for the Indian Viceroyalty, a more appropriate selection could hardly have been made!' Similar instances might easily be multiplied. Sir W. Robertson Nicoll affirms that very few old men look back with regret upon the decisions that they made at the crises of their careers. 'The meaning of that is,' he adds significantly, 'that we are not left so much to our own wisdom as we think. All unconsciously to ourselves we have been guided.' The Kindly Light must be treated very gratefully.

'Up over my table,' writes that most fascinating personage the 'Lady of the Decoration,' 'I have a little picture that you sent me, matey, of the "lane that turned at last." You always said my lane would turn, and it *has*—into a broad road, bordered by cherry blossoms and wisteria.' We have most of us found, somewhere in life, just such an avenue of glorious blossom and delicious fragrance. And as we stroll amidst the loveliness of its petals and the luxury of its perfume, it will do us a world of good to bow our heads and to adore with thankful hearts the Kindly Light that led.

F. W. Boreham, "Lead Kindly Light," *Mountains in the Mist* (London: Charles H. Kelly, 1914), 49-57.

READY-MADE CLOTHES

Carlyle, as everybody knows, once wrote a Philosophy of Clothes, and called it *Sartor Resartus.* He did his work so thoroughly and so exhaustively and so well that, from that day to this, nobody else has cared to tackle the theme. It is high time, however, that it was pointed out that with one important aspect of his tremendous subject he does not attempt to deal. Surely there ought to have been a chapter on Ready-made Clothes!

I am surprised that Henry Drummond never drew attention to the glaring omission, for, if Drummond hated one thing more than another, he loathed and detested ready-made clothes. They were his pet aversion. Ready-made clothes, he used to say, were things that were made to fit everybody, and they fitted nobody. Men are not made by machinery and in sizes; and it follows as a natural consequence that clothes that are so made will not fit men. The man who is an exact duplicate of the tailor's model has not yet been born. How Carlyle's omission escaped the censure of Drummond I cannot imagine. It is true that Drummond was not particularly attracted by Carlyle; he preferred Emerson. I am certain that if Drummond had read *Sartor Resartus* at all carefully he would have exposed the discrepancy, and Carlyle is therefore to be congratulated on a very narrow escape.

Drummond's hatred of ready-made clothes is the essential thing about him. I happened to be lecturing on Drummond the other evening, and I felt it my duty to point out that Drummond would take his place in history, not as a scientist, nor as an evangelist, nor as a traveler, nor as an author, but as the uncompromising and relentless assailant of ready-made clothes. Unless you grasp this, you will never understand him. He scorned all affectations and imitations. He would adopt no style of dress simply because it was usual under certain conditions. 'He was,' as an eyewitness of his ordination remarks, 'the last man whom you could place by the woman's canon of dress. And yet his dress was a marvel of adaptation to the part he happened to be playing. On his ordination day, when most men assume a garb severely clerical, he was dressed like a country squire, thus proclaiming to fathers and brethren, and to all the world, that he was not going to allow ordination to play havoc with his chosen career.' Now this was typical, and it is its typical quality that is important. It applied not to dress alone. It applied to speech. Drummond would affect no style of address simply on the ground that it was usual upon certain platforms or in certain rostrums. Did it fit him? Was it simple, natural, easy, effective? If not, he would not use it. Nor would he adopt a course of procedure simply because it was customary and was considered correct.

If, to him, it seemed like wearing ready-made clothes, he would have none of it. Here you have the key to his whole life. Everything had to fit him like a glove, or he would have nothing to do with it. His scientific lectures, his evangelistic addresses, his personal interviews with students, even his public prayers, were modeled on no regulation standard, on no established precedent; they were couched in the language, and expressed in the style, that most perfectly suited his own charming and magnetic individuality.

Professor James, of Harvard, said of Henri Bergson, the Parisian philosopher, that his utterance fitted his thought like that elastic silk underclothing which follows every movement of his skin. Drummond would have considered that the ideal. Generally speaking, he was impervious to criticism; but if you had told him that a single phrase rang hollow, or that some expression had savored of artificiality, or that even a gesture appeared like affectation, you would have stabbed him to the quick. It was a great question in his day as to whether he was orthodox or heterodox. Drummond regarded all standards of orthodoxy and of heterodoxy as so many tailors' models. Orthodoxy and heterodoxy stand related to truth just as those wonderful wickerwork stands and plaster busts that adorn every dressmaker's establishment stand related to the grace and beauty of the female form. If you had asked Drummond to what school of thought he belonged, he would have told you that he never wore ready-made clothes.

I tremble lest, one of these days, these notions of mine on the subject of ready-made clothes should assume the proportions of a sermon, and demand pulpit utterance. There will at any rate be no difficulty in providing them with a text. The classical instance of the contemptuous rejection of ready-made clothing was, of course, David's refusal to wear Saul's armor. There is a world of significance in that old-world story. Saul's armor is a very fine thing—*for Saul!* But if David feels that he can do better work with a sling, then, in the name of all that is reasonable, give him a sling! If he has to fight Goliath, why hamper him with ready-made clothes? I began by saying that Carlyle omitted to deal, in *Sartor Resartus,* with this profound branch of his subject. But he saw the importance of it for all that. In his *Frederick the Great,* he tells us how the young prince's iron-handed father employed a learned university professor to teach the boy theology. The doctor dosed his youthful pupil with creeds and catechisms until his brain whirled with meaningless tags and phrases. And in recording the story Carlyle bursts out upon the dry-as-dust professor. 'In heaven's name,' he cries, 'teach the boy nothing at all, or else teach him something that he will know, as long as he lives, to be eternally and indisputably true!'

Now what is this fine outburst of thunderous wrath but an emphatic protest against the use of ready-made clothes? A man's faith should fit him like the clothes for which he has been most carefully measured, if not like the elastic silk to which the Harvard professor refers. A man might as well try to wear his father's clothes as try to wear his father's faith. It will never really fit him. There is a great expression near the end of the brief Epistle of Jude that always seems to me very striking. 'But ye, beloved,' says the writer, 'building up yourselves on your most holy faith.'

That is the only satisfactory way of building—to build on your own site. If I build my house on another person's piece of ground, it is sure to cause trouble sooner or later. Build your own character on your own faith, says the apostle; and there is sound sense in the injunction. It is better for me to build a very modest little house of my own on a little bit of land that really belongs to me than to build a palace on somebody else's soil. It is better for me to build up my character, very unpretentiously, perhaps, on my own faith, than to erect a much more imposing structure on another person's creed. That is the philosophy of ready-made clothes, disguised under a slight change of metaphor.

I have heard that some people spend their time in church inspecting other people's clothes. If that is so, they must be profoundly impressed by the amazing proportion of misfits. The souls of thousands are quite obviously clad in ready-made garments. Here is the spirit of a bright young girl decked out in all the contents of her grandmother's spiritual wardrobe. The clothes fitted the grandmother perfectly; the old lady looked charming in them; but the granddaughter looks ridiculous. I was once at a testimony meeting. The thing that most impressed me was the continual repetition of certain phrases. Speaker after speaker rang the changes on the same stereotyped expressions. I saw at once that I had fallen among a people who went in for ready-made clothes.

The thing takes even more objectionable forms. Those who are half as fond as I am of Mark Rutherford will have already recalled Frank Palmer in *Clara Hopgood*. 'He accepted willingly,' we are told, 'the household conclusions on religion and politics, but they were not properly his, for he accepted them merely as conclusions and without the premises, and it was often even a little annoying to hear him express some free opinion on religious questions in a way which showed that it was not a growth, but something picked up.' Everybody who has read the story remembers the moral tragedy that followed. What else could you expect? There is always trouble if a man builds his house on another man's site. The souls of men were never meant to be attired in ready-made clothes. Somebody has finely said that Truth must be born again in the secret silence of each individual life.

For the matter of that, the philosophy of ready-made clothes applies as much to unbelief as to faith. Now and then one meets a mind distracted by genuine doubt, and it is refreshing and stimulating to grapple with its problems. One respects the doubter because the doubt fits him like the elastic silk; it seems a part and parcel of his personality. But at other times one can see at a glance that the doubter is all togged out in ready-made clothes, and, like a bird in borrowed plumes, is inordinately proud of them. Here are the same old questions, put in the same old way, and with a certain effrontery that knows nothing of inner anguish or even deep sincerity. One feels that his visitor has seen this gaudy mental outfit cheaply displayed at the street corner, and has snapped it up at once in order to impress you with the gorgeous spectacle. How often, too, one is made to feel that the blatancy of the infidel lecturer, or the flippancy of the skeptical debater, is simply a matter of ready-made clothes. The awful grandeur of the subjects of which they treat has evidently never appealed to them. They are merely echoing quibbles that are as old as the hills; they are wearing clothes that may have fitted Hobbes, Paine, or Voltaire, but that certainly were not made to fit their more meager stature. Doubt is a very human and a very sacred thing, but the doubt that is merely assumed is, of all affectations, the most repellent.

If some suspicious reader thinks that I am overestimating the danger of wearing ready-made clothes, I need only remind him that even such gigantic humans as James Chalmers, of New Guinea, and Robert Louis Stevenson feared that ready-made clothes might yet stand between the Church and her conquest of the world. Some of the missionaries insisted in clothing the natives of New Guinea in the garb of Old England, but Chalmers protested, and protested vigorously. 'I am opposed to it,' he exclaimed. 'My experience is that clothing natives is nearly as bad as introducing spirits among them. Wherever clothing has been introduced, the natives are disappearing before various diseases, especially consumption, and I am fully convinced that the same will happen in New Guinea. Our civilization, whatever it is, is unfitted for them in their present state, and no attempt should be made to force it upon them.'

With this, Robert Louis Stevenson most cordially concurred. Nobody who knows him will suspect Stevenson of any lack of gallantry, but he always eyed the arrival of the missionary's wife with a certain amount of apprehension. 'The married missionary,' says Stevenson, 'may offer to the native what he is much in want of—a higher picture of domestic life; but the woman at the missionary's elbow tends to keep him in touch with Europe, and out of touch with Polynesia, and threatens to perpetuate, and even to ingrain, parochial decencies far best forgotten. The mind of the lady missionary tends to be continually busied about dress. She can be taught with extreme difficulty to think any costume decent but that to which she grew accustomed on Clapham Common; and to gratify her prejudice, the native is put to useless expense, his mind is tainted with the morbidities of Europe, and his health is set in danger.' We remember the pride with which poor John Williams, the martyr missionary of Erromanga, viewed the introduction of bonnets among the women of Raratonga; but it was not the greatest of his triumphs after all. The bonnets have vanished long ago, but the fragrant influence of John Williams abides perpetually. We sometimes forget that our immaculate tweed trousers and our dainty skirts and blouses are no essential part of the Christian gospel. As a matter of fact, that gospel was first revealed to a people who knew nothing of such trappings. We do not necessarily hasten the millennium by introducing among untutored races a carnival of ready-made clothes.

And it is just as certain that you do not bring the soul nearer to its highest goal by forcing on it a fashion for which it is totally unsuited. And here I come back to Drummond. During his last illness at Tunbridge Wells, he remarked that, at the age of twelve, he made a conscientious study of Bonar's *God's Way of Peace.* 'I fear,' he said, 'that the book did me more harm than good. I tried to force my inner experience into the mold represented by that book, and it was impossible.' In one of Moody's after-meetings in London, Drummond was dealing with a young girl who was earnestly seeking the Savior. At last he startled her by exclaiming, 'You must give up reading James's *Anxious Enquirer.*' She wondered how he had guessed that she had been reading it; but he had detected from her conversation that she was making his earlier mistake. She was trying to think as

John Angell James thought, to weep as he wept, and to find her way to faith precisely as he found his. Drummond told her to read nothing but the New Testament, and, he said later on, 'A fortnight of that put her right!' There lies the whole secret. Our souls no more resemble each other than our bodies; they are not made in a mold and turned out by the million. No two are exactly alike. Ready-made clothes will never exactly fit. Bonar and James, Bunyan and Law, Doddridge and Wesley, Mullet and Spurgeon, may help me amazingly. They may help me by showing me how they—each for himself—found their way into the presence of the Eternal and, like Christian at the Palace Beautiful, were robed and armed for pilgrimage. But if they lead me to suppose that I must experience their sensations, enjoy their elations, pass through their depressions, struggle and laugh and weep and sing just as they did, they have done me serious damage. They have led me away from those secret chambers in which the King adorns the soul in beautiful and comely garments, and they have left me a mere wearer of ready-made clothes.

F. W. Boreham, "Ready-made Clothes," *Mushrooms on the Moor* (London: Charles H. Kelly, 1915), 21-32.

ABRAHAM LINCOLN'S TEXT

I

The massive personality of Abraham Lincoln is like a granite boulder torn from a rugged hillside. Too gigantic to be localized, he bursts all the bounds of nationality and takes his place in history as a huge cosmopolite. He belongs, as Edwin Stanton so finely exclaimed, in announcing that the last breath of the assassinated President had been drawn, he belongs henceforth to the ages! With the fine stroke and gesture of a king, he piloted the civilization of the West through the most momentous crisis of its history; and, in doing so, he established principles which will stand as the landmarks of statecraft as long as the world endures.

He was an immense human. As Edwin Markham sings:

The color of the ground was in him, the red earth;
The smack and tang of elemental things;
The rectitude and patience of the cliff;

The goodwill of the rain that loves all leaves;
The friendly welcome of the wayside well;
The courage of the bird that dares the sea;
The gladness of the wind that shakes the corn;
The pity of the snow that hides all scars.

Some men are far mightier than their achievements. What they *do* is great; but what they *are* is infinitely greater. Abraham Lincoln is the outstanding example of the men of this towering and gigantic cast. The world contains millions of people who know little of American history, and who have but the haziest notions as to the issues at stake in the Civil War, yet upon whose ears the name of Abraham Lincoln falls like an encrusted tradition, like a golden legend, like a brave, inspiring song.

For one thing, we all seem to have seen him. We are extraordinarily familiar with his long, lean, sallow face; his leathery cheeks; his large, protruding ears; his dreamy, melancholy eyes; his tumbled, wayward hair; his six-feet-four of bony awkwardness. At the mere mention of his name, that gawky, angular, and ill-proportioned form—long arms, long legs, enormous hands and feet—garbed in the clothes that never seem to fit, shambles its uncouth way before our eyes. His coats were the despair of his tailor, and his battered hats nearly broke the heart of his wife. In more ways than one, Lincoln was terribly handicapped. In temperament, as well as in appearance, he had much to overcome. At the outset of his career he was not only unattractive and illiterate, he was self-opinionated, overbearing, and abominably ill-mannered. Women, especially, were repelled by him. One lady told him frankly that he was never ready with those little gracious acts and attentions which ladies so highly and so rightly value, though, in the next breath, she admitted that he had a heart full of kindness and a head full of common sense. The anecdotes that lent piquancy to his earlier speeches were too coarse to be printed. In a word, he was, in those days, scarcely a gentleman. It is only against this background that we can properly appreciate his triumph. He developed an infinite capacity for self-culture. Awaking to the fact that he was boorish, clumsy, and unpleasing, he set himself steadfastly to work to remedy these formidable defects. To this severe task he applied himself so successfully that he became, in the end, one of the most finished orators of his time, one of the most powerful statesmen that the world has ever seen, and one of the most perfect gentlemen that any society could desire.

And, beyond the shadow of a doubt, it was by means of his faith that he did it. His faith, it has been said, was not of the orthodox type. Nor were his features. But his faith, like his features, suited *him*. In a famous ode, Lowell sings of the sublime simplicity of Lincoln's faith; it produced, he says, 'the brave old wisdom of sincerity.' Emerson holds that the majestic simplicity of Lincoln's faith is the subtle secret that alone explains the splendor of his eloquence. Tolstoy describes him as 'a miniature Christ,' while Father Chiniquy, a Roman Catholic, found in him the most perfect type of Christian.

In view of all this, an analysis of the rise and progress of Lincoln's faith is particularly alluring. It divides itself into three distinct phases. There is the *Iron Age* of his faith; there is the *Age of Clay;* and there is the *Golden Age.* Each is worth a glance.

II

Lincoln climbed Mount Sinai with Moses: that was how the *Iron Age* began. He was born in the midst of that tumultuous religious upheaval—that backwoods revival—which stands inseparably connected with the name of Peter Cartwright. He was, in a peculiar sense, the child of the camp-meeting. A tradition, cited by Judge Herndon, declares that, a few years before his birth, a certain camp-meeting had been in progress for several clays. Religious fervor ran at fever heat. Gathered in complete accord, the company awaited with awed intensity the falling of the celestial fire. Suddenly the camp was stirred. Something extraordinary had happened. The kneeling multitude sprang to its feet and broke into shouts which rang through the primeval shades. A young man, who had been absorbed in prayer, began leaping, dancing, and shouting. Simultaneously, a young woman sprang forward, her hat falling to the ground, her hair tumbling about her shoulders in graceful braids, her eyes fixed heavenwards, her lips vocal with strange, unearthly song. Her rapture increased until, grasping the hand of the young man, they blended their voices in ecstatic melody. These two, the record assures us, were married a week later, and became the parents of Abraham Lincoln.

By the time that the boy had reached years of intelligent observation, however, this strange movement had changed its character. It became ethical rather than emotional. Even Peter Cartwright devoted himself to rebuking the political corruptions and commercial depravities that were eating into the heart of society. The red-hot propaganda of an earlier day crystallized into a passionate insistence upon national and individual righteousness.

Abraham Lincoln's young mother died when he was barely nine. Her husband had to nurse her, close her eyes, make her coffin, and dig her grave. Abraham helped him carry that melancholy burden from the desolated cabin to its lonely resting-place in the woods. He never forgot that mother of his. 'All that I am,' he used to say, 'my angel-mother made me!' And the memory that lingered longest was the thought of her as she sat in the old log-cabin teaching him the *Ten Commandments*. Many a time afterwards, when he was asked how he had found the courage to decline some tempting bribe, or to resist some particularly insidious suggestion, he said that, in the critical hour, he heard his mother's voice repeating once more the old, old words: '*I am the Lord thy God; thou shalt have no other gods before Me.*' He treasured all through life her last words:

> I am going away from you, Abraham, and shall not return [she said]. I know that you will be a good boy, and that you will be kind to your father. I want you to live as I have taught you, to love your Heavenly Father and to keep His commandments.

'*Keep His commandments.*' It was thus that, in infancy, Abraham Lincoln climbed Mount Sinai. It was thus that the Iron Age of his religious history was inaugurated. As a result, somebody said of him that he was the most honest lawyer west of China. 'He was quite indifferent to money,' as Mr. A. C. Benson points out; 'he defended poor clients for nothing, and would even remind opposing counsel of points against his own case which they had overlooked.' This phase of his spiritual pilgrimage was *augmented;* it was never *obliterated.* Christ comes into the soul not to destroy, but to fulfill, the law. Lincoln's earliest religious impressions imparted to his character a severity that contributed materially to its grandeur.

III

Lincoln climbed Mount Carmel with Elijah; that was how the *Age of Clay*—the plastic age—began. Elijah learned on Mount Carmel that his loneliness in the midst of unscrupulous foes mattered little so long as the God who Answers by Fire was with him. Lincoln learned identically the same lesson when, in 1860, he left his old home at Springfield and turned his face towards Washington. It was for him the hour of destiny. President McKinley has told us how, in that fateful hour, Lincoln received a flag from one of his admirers. On its silken folds he read, beautifully worked, the words: '*Be strong and of a good courage; be not afraid, neither be thou dismayed: for the Lord thy God is with thee whithersoever thou goest. There shall not any man be able to stand before thee all the days of thy life. As I was with Moses, so shall I be with thee.'*

The words inscribed on the flag became the keynote of this *second* phase of his experience. He was going to Washington to assume the Presidency. He felt—and said—that he was as much and as truly called to lead the American people as Moses was called to lead the Hebrew people. He regarded himself as a Man with a Mission. Indeed, he had *two* missions—one immediate and one remote. The *immediate* mission was the preservation of the Union; the *remote* mission was the abolition of slavery. On both issues he was in deadly earnest; for either cause he was prepared to die. And he knew perfectly well that death was not improbable. Plots were laid to assassinate him before he could reach Washington. But he never wavered; the words on the flag were constantly in his mind. At every wayside station crowds gathered to greet him. And Dr. Hill points out that, in addressing each of these groups, he declared emphatically that he was going forth in the name of the Living God. 'Not even Moses praying in the wilderness: "*If Thy presence go not with me, carry me not up hence,*" seemed more dependent on the divine aid than did Lincoln as he slowly journeyed to Washington.'

In accepting the Presidency, Lincoln was very sure of God. It meant two things to him. It meant that he would be protected, sustained, directed, and prospered in his lofty enterprise; he was immortal until his work was done. But it meant more. He was intensely, almost painfully, conscious of his own disqualifications and disabilities. He was a backwoodsman on his way to White House! But he believed that—according to the promise on the flag—God was with him. Like Moses, he would be clay in the hands of the divine Potter; and, by those Unseen Hands, he would be molded and shaped and fashioned. Here lies the secret of that ceaseless development and complete transformation which, as Lord Charnwood says, is the most amazing thing about him. It is for this reason that I have called this second phase the *Age of Clay.* It is the plastic, pliable, formative period of Lincoln's inner life. Yet it is by no means the climax.

IV

Lincoln climbed Mount Calvary with John: that was how the *Golden Age* began. But before Calvary comes Gethsemane; and certainly Lincoln passed through that Garden of Anguish. Mr. H. C. Whitney says that, during the war, Lincoln's companions would leave him by the fireside at night and find him still there—elbows on knees and face in hands—when they came down in the morning. *'Father,'* he would moan again and again, *'Father, if it be possible, let this cup pass from me!'* Late one Sunday night he called on Henry Ward Beecher, looking 'so bowed with care, so broken by the sorrows of the nation,' that it was difficult even to recognize him. A look of unutterable weariness had crept into his sunken eyes. 'I think,' he confided to a friend, 'I think I shall never be glad again.' Yet, as Dr. Hill points out, it was this discipline of suffering that rendered his faith irresistible and triumphant. But how?

The greatest grief of his life was the death of his son. As the boy lay dying, Lincoln's reason seemed in peril. Miss Ida Tarbell has told the sad story with great delicacy and judgement. When the dread blow fell, the nurse and the father stood with bowed heads beside the dead boy, and then the nurse, out of her own deep experience of human sorrow and of divine comfort, pointed the weeping President to her Savior.

The work that this *private* sorrow began the *public* sorrow completed. Lincoln had long yearned for a fuller, sweeter, more satisfying faith. 'I have been reading the Beatitudes,' he tells a friend, 'and can at least claim the blessing that is pronounced upon those who *hunger and thirst after righteousness.*' He was to hunger no longer. A few days before his death he told of the way in which the peace of heaven stole in his heart. 'When I left Springfield,' he said, not without a thought of the flag and its inscription, 'when I left Springfield, I asked the people to pray for me; I was not a Christian. When I buried my son—the severest trial of my life—I was not a Christian. But when I went to Gettysburg, and saw the graves of thousands of our soldiers, I then and there consecrated myself to Christ.' From that moment, Dr. Hill says, the habitual attitude of the mind was expressed in the words: '*God be merciful to me, a sinner!*' With tears in his eyes he told his friends that he had at last found the faith that he had longed for. He realized, he said, that his heart was changed, and that he loved the Savior. The President was at the Cross!

V

Happily, he lived to see the sunshine that followed the storm. He lived to see Peace and Union and Emancipation triumphant. His last hours were spent amid services of thanksgiving and festivals of rejoicing. One of these celebrations was being held in Ford's Theatre at Washington. The President was there, and attracted as much attention as the actors. But his mind was not on the play. Indeed, it was nearly over when he arrived. He leaned forward, talking, under his breath, to Mrs. Lincoln. Now that the war was over, he said, he would like to take her for a tour of the East. They would visit Palestine—would see Gethsemane and Calvary—would walk together the streets of Jerusalem.

But, before the word was finished, a pistol-shot—the 'maddest pistol-shot in the history of the ages'—rang through the theater. And he who had climbed Mount Sinai with Moses, Mount Carmel with Elijah, and Mount Calvary with John, had turned his pilgrim feet towards the holiest heights of all.

F. W. Boreham, "Abraham Lincoln's Text," *A Temple of Topaz* (London: The Epworth Press, 1928), 22-32.

THE LONG ARM OF COINCIDENCE

No man should think seriously of dying until he has committed to paper a list of the most striking and extraordinary coincidences that have come under his personal observation. I do not mean those of which he has read. As I have tried to demonstrate in *A Reel of Rainbow,* the stately coincidences of history are tremendously impressive and dramatic. But they are common property: anyone can collate them. In the course of each man's personal pilgrimage, however, he encounters a few combinations of circumstances so arbitrary, so fortuitous and so bewildering as to be almost freakish. Were a novelist to weave them into the web of his romance, the reviewers would charge him with having transgressed all the bounds of probability. His plot would be condemned as a flagrant outrage of the literary canons. Yet these things actually happened! If each man were to recall and record such surprising experiences while it is still in his power to do so, some very valuable and practical purposes would be served.

Let me crystallize my abstract doctrine into concrete example by a few instances of the kind of thing I have in mind. I will begin with my wedding-day. We were married at Kaiapoi, New Zealand, early in the morning and caught that day's express for the south. A friend, knowing of our movements, sent a congratulatory telegram to the train. The guard handed it to me—opened!

'Very sorry, sir,' he murmured, 'but there's another young couple of the same name in the next carriage!'

In view of the fact that my name is not a particularly common one, an involuntary doubt sprang to my mind; but, later on, we met our namesakes, who were most profuse in their apologies.

Or take another case. I have lived, roughly, about twenty-five thousand days. On only one of those days have I been bitten by a dog; but on that memorable day I was bitten *by two*. I had set out to visit a friend who lived about three miles from my own home. As I turned into his street, an infuriated dog rushed out of an open gate and savagely attacked me, fastening his teeth into my leg. Somewhat shaken, I managed to reach my friend's house, where my wound was bathed and bandaged. An hour later I set out for home, and, almost within sight of it, was assailed by another dog and again bitten. Puzzled by the unwonted attention paid me that day by the canine tribe, I carefully examined everything about my person—my clothing, my walking-stick and the contents of my pockets. But everything was perfectly normal. Men deeply versed in the mentality of dogs have suggested that the first attack had affected my nerve and that the second dog had sensed in me an attitude of apprehension and distrust which, awakening his resentment, laid me open to further victimization. I do not know. The plausible theory is sound or it is unsound. If it is sound, then the astonishing thing is that I have passed unbitten by every dog that I have since met. If it is unsound, then my brace of bites remain among life's inexplicable coincidences.

On a beautiful summer's evening in 1924 I was enjoying, with a party of congenial friends, a delightful drive across the Devonshire moors. On the far horizon we suddenly descried a puff of dust out of which, as we drew nearer, there emerged a man with a few sheep: it must have been market-day at a nearby moorland town. As soon as we could determine the nature of the objects that had created the cloud, a mischievous mood fell upon me.

'Ah,' I observed, casually, 'here comes a man with seventeen sheep!'

'Seventeen!' exclaimed my companions in astonishment. 'How on earth can you count them at this distance? It is difficult to see the sheep for the dust!'

We drove on, and, in due course, met the flock. I could scarcely believe my eyes when it became clear that the sheep numbered exactly seventeen. I carried off the situation with a fine assumption of visual and mathematical superiority, deriding my companions on their pitiable blindness. But within half an hour, to my discomfiture, we made out another, and much larger, mob of sheep.

'Well,' exclaimed my friend beside me, 'you were very clever in counting the animals in the first flock: how many are there in *this* one?' It was a case of neck or nothing and I resolved to go down with all flags flying.

'Do you mean to say,' I replied, 'that you really cannot count those sheep? Why, man, it's as plain as a pikestaff that there are a hundred and nineteen of them!'

Shall I ever forget the speechless stupefaction that I struggled to conceal when, on meeting the sheep, we learned from the drover that they numbered a hundred and nineteen precisely?

In 1936 my wife and I were occupying a room on the fourth floor of the Cumberland Hotel, facing the Marble Arch in Hyde Park, London. The Australian mail one morning brought a letter from our daughter.

'Do you know,' she asked, 'that Carl Fairfax is in London? I wonder if you will run across him!'

I smiled inwardly at the vast improbability, during the few days that remained to us, of our meeting this solitary Australian amid the maze of London's millions. With the letter still in my hand I stepped out of the bedroom on to the lift. And the only person on the lift was Carl Fairfax!

With a number of cricket companions I was one Saturday afternoon watching the final football match of the winter. It was being played on the Melbourne Cricket Ground; but we ourselves were far less interested in the play that we were watching than in the Test Match that, in a few hours' time, was to be played at the Kennington Oval. It was the match on which the Ashes depended, and we were eagerly anticipating the ball-to-ball description to which we would be listening in the evening. During the half-time interval in the football, somebody suggested that, on the assumption that Australia batted first, we should each attempt to forecast the score at the close of the first day's play. A paper was passed round: each of us was to state a figure and initial it.

When the document fell into my hands, I noticed that the estimates of my predecessors ranged from 250 to 350 runs. I was just setting myself to frame some kind of conjecture when the absurdity of the whole thing broke upon me. We had no idea as to what the wicket was like, or the weather, or any of the conditions on which scoring depended. So, in the same impish and irresponsible mood in which I had feigned to count the sheep, I scribbled 475 and passed the paper on.

'Four hundred and seventy-five!' cried the man who had set us the grotesquely impossible task; 'why, if Australia has four hundred and seventy-five runs on the board at the end of the first day's play, you'll be so excited that you'll announce hymn No. 475 instead of the proper hymn when you enter the pulpit tomorrow morning!'

To my sober judgement the figure seemed as fantastic as it did to his. But, believe it or not, 475 was the Australian score when stumps were drawn that night at the Oval; and, when I entered the vestry at Footscray next morning and the hymn list was handed to me, I discovered that the service was to commence with *Glorious things of thee are spoken—No. 475!*

Any man who cares to ransack the pigeon-holes of his memory will find a wealthy hoard of such recollections stowed away there. They teach him charity. For, obviously, it does not follow, because several circumstances happen to point steadily in one direction, that the conclusion suggested by their unanimity is necessarily established. What seems like corroboration may be pure coincidence. And surely they make faith less difficult. For if, among the ordinary odds and ends of life, we find ourselves confronted by situations so remarkable as to be almost incredible, it is by no means surprising that, in a more august and mysterious realm, we sometimes find ourselves out of our depth.

I turn from these coincidences, which are *pure* coincidences, to those remarkable happenings, familiar to us all, beneath the surface of which we seem to sense something that is *more* than mere coincidence. How often, in walking down the street, you find your thoughts suddenly and irresistibly reverting to the memory of a friend whom you have not seen for months, perhaps for years. Within five minutes you turn a corner and meet him face to face! It is easy to wave such incidents aside with an airy reference to telepathy. That blessed word 'telepathy' is a hot rival to that blessed word 'Mesopotamia.' What is telepathy?

And then again, the confident conclusions of the spiritualists can only be met by a frank recognition of the fact that, behind the forces that Science has investigated and classified, there are other forces, shadowy and elusive, that, so far, we have only vaguely sensed. I am intimate with a family—devoutly Christian and by no means superstitious—in whose home a thing occurred one evening that set every member of the household thinking of a very dear relative on the other side of the world. At the very hour of that singular happening, that relative died. Since scores of people die in England every day to whose kinsfolk in Australia no such mysterious intimation is vouchsafed, the episode was evidently the operation of no fixed law. It proves nothing. Yet the comparative frequency of such enigmatical incidents makes us feel with Hamlet that:

> There are more things in heaven and earth, Horatio,
> Than are dreamt of in your philosophy.

These evasive and abstruse events must be numbered among life's strange and striking coincidences; and yet they leave behind them an impression that, woven into the very texture of their being, there is something that lifts them above the level of mere coincidences.

Only last night I came upon a set of circumstances so arresting and so intriguing that, for the life of me, I cannot with confidence declare that they do, or do not, represent anything more than a very remarkable coincidence.

I number among my friends two young ladies—Beryl Hamilton and Lucy Minogue—who, as partners, control one of those attractive businesses whose windows and counters are tastefully adorned with high-class bric-á-brac—artistic pottery, pretty paintings, dainty calendars, busts, plaques, statuettes, and the like. Beryl is a Protestant, Lucy a Catholic. Both are transparently sincere, and each is the soul of courtesy and consideration in her attitude towards the faith of the other.

Some time ago, Lucy's mother, a widow, to whom she was passionately devoted, suddenly died. The cruel shock and the desolating loss shattered the daughter's nerve. Night and day, she could think of nothing but her dead mother. Where was she? Would they ever meet again and be to each other what they had been in the old days? And, above all, was her mother happy? The sacraments of her Church comforted her, but they gave her no solid satisfaction on this point. Was her mother happy? How could she ascertain? The terrible uncertainty, preying constantly upon her mind, affected her health; and Beryl, her partner, urged her to take a good rest with an entire change of scene.

'Why not go to Sydney?' Beryl pleaded. 'A quiet spot in the country or beside the sea might give you too much time to brood. But Sydney is a lovely place for a holiday. You will have the city to distract your thoughts when you desire that kind of relaxation, and, whenever you feel inclined for the beach or the bush, you can find a new excursion every day. It will do you heaps of good. And I'll be quite all right here. It's the slack season, and either of us could easily be spared.'

Infected by Beryl's enthusiasm, Lucy agreed to do so. And it was during that visit to Sydney that she encountered the experience of which I am about to tell.

She thoroughly enjoyed her stay and was particularly appreciative of the good sense displayed by her partner in suggesting the venue of her holiday. Beneath all her pleasure, however, she was subconsciously aware of the old deep undertone of terrible loneliness and insatiable longing. If only she knew—knew for certain—that all was well with her mother! Impelled by some such mood, she one afternoon turned from the bustle of the city to rest quietly for a while amid the green lawns and gushing fountains and colorful flower-beds of Hyde Park. Seated there, her eye came to rest on the graceful turrets and Gothic stateliness of St. Mary's Cathedral. As though magnetized by its solemn splendor, she rose and turned her footsteps towards it.

In wandering aimlessly but meditatively about the Cathedral, she felt herself drawn—she scarcely knew why—towards a small statue of Santa Teresa. It instantly brought to mind the lovely stories that her mother had told her. Her mother always spoke of Santa Teresa as the most human, the most understanding, the most womanly of saints—a saint who radiated sympathy and courage and common sense. She used to tell Lucy of Teresa's fondness, as an old woman, for the young nuns under her charge and of her anxiety that they should all be perfectly happy. Lucy had never before seen a representation of Santa Teresa; but now that she looked into her sculptured face, she felt that there was something singularly winsome and kindly in her countenance. Teresa was represented, in the statue, as carrying a cross and an armful of roses. Why the flowers? Lucy wondered.

A pair of nuns had glided silently up the Cathedral aisles, and, the movements of the elder of the two having been arrested by a question from an attendant, the younger moved slowly on and was waiting for her companion at a spot close to Lucy's elbow.

'You are interested in Saint Teresa?' asked the young nun, in slightly foreign but strangely musical accents.

'I was wondering why she is represented as carrying flowers,' Lucy replied with diffidence.

'Saint Teresa loved flowers—roses particularly,' explained the pale-faced nun. 'She planted red roses all round the grounds of her Convent at Avila, and, whenever she desired to bestow any signal favor upon any of her young nuns, she invariably accompanied it with the gift of a red rose.'

By this time the elder nun had approached, and, with the softest suspicion of a smile, the pair moved on, leaving Lucy alone with the statue.

'Oh, Santa Teresa,' Lucy sighed rather than prayed, for she remained standing and open-eyed, 'oh, Santa Teresa, the condition of my dear, dear mother must be known to thee. If only thou could'st send me a red rose to tell me of her blessedness! If only thou could'st—and would'st!'

That afternoon, in Melbourne, Beryl was writing to her friend. Lucy was not to worry, Beryl said, everything at the shop was going well. 'Make the most of your holiday; stay as long as you can; and come back all smiles.' She was just about to seal the letter when her eye fell upon the vase of flowers with which she had decorated her desk. Almost mechanically she took a small red rose, pressed it, folded it in tissue paper and slipped it into the envelope.

And when, next day, Lucy opened the letter, she was unable to read it. At sight of the red rose, she sobbed as though her heart would break. But her tears were tears of joy and gratitude. And from that moment she never grieved again.

Was it purely a coincidence, *purely* a coincidence? Was it? I wonder! Who shall say?

And there is a third class of coincidences. Here, for example, are a number of people gathered together in the house of John Mark in Jerusalem. Peter is in prison and these good men and women have met to pray for him. And, while they pray, a great light illumines the darkness of the dungeon. Angels appear: chains fall: gates fly open: Peter escapes!

Every person of any spiritual experience at all has met with such coincidences. One has prayed and things have happened. One has been profoundly moved to write a certain letter or to pay a certain visit. The letter or the visit proved to be the very thing that the grateful recipient most sorely needed. Or one has been perplexed; has sought guidance; and, 'o'er moor and fen, o'er crag and torrent,' the

Kindly Light has led in the most wonderful way. When we approach these sublime coincidences, we shed our sense of surprise and yield instead to adoration. We feel that we are merely beholding, on the most exalted plane, the operation of the law of cause and effect. The forces at work in producing the coinciding factors are so obvious that we no longer consider the resultant coincidences as coincidences at all.

F. W. Boreham, "The Long Arm of Coincidence," *I Forgot to Say* (London: The Epworth Press, 1939), 87-96.

ON CLIMBING DOWN

Courage never shines so lustrously as when it is in full retreat. A dramatic and brilliant charge must be a soul-stirring affair; but, in the nature of things, few of us can ever hope for the opportunity of covering ourselves with glory under such thrilling and romantic circumstances. I never expect in this world—or in any other—to find myself participating in a maneuver so exciting. But I have my compensations. For, every day of my life, I find myself under the humiliating necessity of executing a retreat. In the genial glow of every fireside argument I assume positions that, as the controversy develops, I see to be utterly untenable; in the rush and bustle of life I say and do things that, on leisurely reflection, fill me with profound regret; in waves of sudden enthusiasm, or in gusts of sudden indignation, I commit myself to courses that, in the hush of twilight, I see to be tactless and futile; I even commit myself in writing to statements that I subsequently discover to be unjustifiable. These are the cheerless situations that provide most of us—creatures of common clay—with the opportunity to display genuine gallantry. It is by the skill with which we extricate ourselves from such positions that we achieve distinction. There is no acrobatic performance that offers such scope to the aspiring gymnast as the feat usually described as *climbing down*. It is when a man is in full retreat that he enjoys the most sublime opportunity of proving himself a hero.

A coward never retreats. Having once taken up a position, he clings desperately to it, although he grimly feels that its occupation must prove his ultimate undoing. '*What I have written, I have written,*' exclaims Pilate, with a fine assumption of boldness, even while, in the profundities of his soul, a thousand voices are crying out in protest, and he secretly wishes that he had never put his hand to the fatal document. Pilate is by no means alone. We are all familiar with the politician who, finding himself in doubt as to one of the planks of his party's platform, yet dreading the displeasure of his leaders and associates, makes a bolder statement of his policy than ever, and assures himself that he is once more on firm ground. He assumes a note of emphasis to cloak his torments of uncertainty. It is the behavior of the boy who whistles to keep his courage up.

In order that we may have one or two concrete cases before us, let me pillory a pair of illustrious offenders. The one is from Kingsley's *Water-Babies;* the other is from Le Sage's *Gil Blas.*

Professor Ptthmllnsprt was, Kingsley assures us, a very eminent naturalist. Indeed, at the meetings of the British Association held in Melbourne, Australia, in 1899, he had read a very learned paper in which he had conclusively proved that there were no such things as Water-Babies. Not long afterwards, he and little Ellie were paddling about at the seaside, dragging the pools with a hand-net. All at once the net became very heavy, and there, entangled in the meshes, was a Water-Baby!

'Dear me,' cried the professor, 'what a large pink Holothurian; with hands, too! It must be connected with Synapta!' And he took him out of the water.

'It has actually eyes!' he continued. 'Why, it must be a Cephalopod! This is most extraordinary!'

'It's a Water-Baby!' cried Ellie; and of course it was.

'Water-fiddlesticks, my dear!' said the professor; and he turned away sharply. There was no denying it. It *was* a Water-Baby; and he had declared emphatically that no such things existed! What was he to do? He would have liked to have kept the Water-Baby; to have called him Hydrotecnon Ptthmllnsprtsianum, or some other long name like that, and to have bragged about his wonderful discovery for the rest of his days. But that would never do. What would all the learned men say to him after his speech at the British Association? And what would Ellie say? No, no; there was nothing for it but to let the Water-Baby go, and to invent a lot of long words with which to explain him.

'Now,' says Kingsley, 'if the professor had said to Ellie: "Yes, my darling, it is a Water-Baby, and a very wonderful thing, to be sure. It shows how little I know of the wonders of Nature, in spite of forty years' honest labor. I was just telling you that there could be no such creature; and, behold, here is one come to confound my conceit and show me that Nature can do, and has done, more than man's poor fancy can imagine. So let us thank the Lord of Nature for all His wonderful and glorious works, and try and find out something about this one!"—if, Kingsley says, 'the professor had talked like that, little Ellie would have believed him more firmly, and respected him more deeply, and loved him better than she had ever done before.' But the poor professor lacked the pluck. '*What I have written, I have written,*' he muttered. He was too great a coward to retreat. And so he missed his one and only chance of adding a deathless luster to his name.

Turning to the other case, it will be remembered that Gil Blas was apprenticed to the celebrated Dr. Sangrado, one of the most eminent practitioners in Spain. The singular thing was, however, that Dr. Sangrado had one sovereign remedy for maladies of every kind; and all that he and Gil Blas had to do was to hurry from bedside to bedside applying that potent panacea. The thing that troubled Gil Blas most was the fact that, without an exception, all his patients died. He took his master into his confidence and discovered that he was having an identically similar experience. Gil Blas modestly suggested that they should modify their method of treatment.

'I would willingly do so,' replied Dr. Sangrado, 'provided that it would have no bad consequence; but I have published a book in which I have exalted this wonderful system; and wouldst thou have me decry my own work?'

'You are right,' replied the complaisant Gil Blas, 'you must not give your enemies such a triumph over you. It would completely ruin your great reputation. Perish, rather, the people, the nobility, and the clergy! Let us continue in our old path!'

The same timidity takes other forms. In *The Everlasting Mercy*, Mr. John Masefield has revealed a flash of profound psychological and spiritual insight in making Saul Kane blaspheme more loudly, and sin more blatantly, after he became the subject of deep religious convictions. Mr. Masefield's poem is in line with the classical records of all great spiritual experiences. The soul instinctively recoils from the thought of self-repudiation. It rebels against retreat.

But why? Some of the most glorious pages in military history are the records of retreats. The retreat from Mons and the evacuation of Gallipoli represent two of the most stirring stories of the recent war. It is often so. When Dr. Johnson visited Plymouth, many of the citizens crowded about him, eager to enjoy the privilege of conversation with so wonderful a man. Among these, Boswell tells us, was a lady who had so profound a veneration for the doctor that she always supposed him endowed with infallibility. She had been puzzled, however, by the circumstance that, in his famous dictionary, Dr. Johnson defines the word *pastern* as the *knee of a horse*. Approaching the object of her reverence, she nervously stated her difficulty, expecting to hear an explanation drawn from some deeply learned source with which she was unacquainted. To her astonishment, however, instead of making an elaborate defence, the doctor at once replied: 'Ignorance, madam, pure ignorance!' He was too great a man to adopt the flimsy tactics of poor Professor Ptthmllnsprt. It was by his absolute candor and his transparent honesty that he made people trust and love him. The old doctor would have snorted in fine scorn at the pitiful cowardice that is ashamed or afraid to retreat.

Let nobody suppose that I cited old Professor Ptthmllnsprt and poor Dr. Sangrado as typical examples of the scientific temper. By no means! In the course of his presidential address before the British Association, Sir Michael Foster outlined the qualifications that represent the essentials of a distinctively scientific spirit. One is *absolute truthfulness;* another *is moral courage.* Professor Ptthmllnsprt and Dr. Sangrado possessed neither. A true scientist, like Darwin, exhibits both. Through long years of patient investigation, Darwin would discover that thousands of specimens, in given circumstances, behave in a particular way. The evidence would appear overwhelming; but, just as he was about to generalize on these harmonious observations, and to announce his conclusion, he would suddenly come upon a specimen that, under identically similar conditions, behaved in a different way. It would have been the easiest thing in the world to have dismissed the awkward phenomenon with the cheap sophistry that the exception proves the rule. But so plausible a way of escape is inconsistent with the best traditions of scientific research, and the premature conclusion was immediately abandoned as untenable. 'The little beast is doing just what I did not want him to do!' Darwin would exclaim; and, impregnable as his position had seemed, he would evacuate it with dignity and honor.

In his life of his father, Sir Francis Darwin tells a charming and characteristic story. It happened that Mr. G. J. Romanes, the Canadian scientist, was the guest of Darwin. The evening had been spent by Darwin, Romanes, and the younger Darwin in discussing by the fireside a variety of questions, including the ability of magnificent scenery to awaken emotions of reverence. Darwin remarked incidentally that he had never experienced that sensation so powerfully as when standing on the slopes of the Cordilleras.

A little later the old scientist retired for the night, leaving his guest and his son by the fire. Two or three hours afterwards the door opened, and the elder Darwin, in dressing-gown and slippers, re-entered the room. 'Lying in bed,' he explained, 'I have come to the conclusion that I was wrong in what I said just now. I experienced the sensation of reverence, inspired by natural scenery, most of all in the forests of Brazil. I could not sleep until I had corrected myself. It might conceivably affect your conclusions.'

It was a small thing; a mere matter of personal taste and judgement; but the old man, true to the last to the traditions of science, felt that his memory had betrayed him into a false position, and he could not sleep until he had effected a graceful and honorable retreat.

Grant Allen bears similar testimony to Sir Charles Lyell. All through the years he taught a certain theory of the universe. Then, towards the end, new light dawned upon him. He saw clearly that his interpretation of things was entirely mistaken. Should he therefore repudiate all that he had taught, and condemn the books that, with such care, he had written? It would have been the easiest thing in the world to behave as Professor Ptthmllnsprt behaved. The temptation to say with Pilate '*What I have written, I have written*' was very strong. But he knew a more excellent way. 'He nobly ranged himself,' Grant Allen says, 'on the side of what his intellect judged to be the truth of nature, though his emotions urged him hard to blind his judgement and to neglect its light. Science has no more pathetic figure than that of the old philosopher, in his sixty-sixth year, throwing himself with all the eagerness of youth into what he had long considered the wrong scale, and vigorously wrecking the very foundations of his beloved creed. But still he did it. He came out and was separate. Deep as was the pang that the recantation cost him, he formally retracted his earlier works and accepted the theory that he had so often and so deliberately rejected.' It was a noble retreat.

Nor is the Church without examples of the same lofty type of moral heroism. 'Listen, good people,' cries Archbishop Cranmer, on being condemned to death for heresy, 'listen! Forasmuch as I am come to the last end of life, one thing troubleth my conscience more than anything that ever I did or said; and that is the setting abroad of a writing contrary to the truth, which writing I here and now renounce and refuse.' He referred to the recantation by means of which, in a weak moment, he had once escaped a cruel death. 'And,' he continued, 'forasmuch as my *hand* hath offended, writing contrary to my heart, therefore my *hand* shall first be punished; for, when I come to the fire, it shall first be burned.' He was as good as his word. For, says Foxe, 'when the wood was kindled, and the fire began to burn near him, he stretched forth into the flame his right hand, and there held it steadfastly, that the people might see it burned to a coal before his body was touched.'

And what of Thomas Chalmers? When little more than a boy, and before his great spiritual illumination came to him, he had declared that one day a week was ample for the discharge of a minister's tasks of pulpit preparation and pastoral visitation. Many years afterwards, in a great debate in the General Assembly, a prominent speaker used the same argument, and quoted Chalmers. Amidst a death-like stillness, the great man rose to reply. 'Sir,' he exclaimed, 'that sentence was penned in my unregenerate ignorance and pride. I was at that time more devoted to mathematical science than to the literature of my profession. Strangely blinded that I was! What, sir, is the object of mathematical science? Magnitude and the proportions of magnitude. But then, sir, I had forgotten two magnitudes. I thought not of the littleness of time; I recklessly thought not of the greatness of eternity!'

Eternity! In the light of that word any man may be pardoned for retracting his hasty utterances, reviewing his aims and aspirations, and even recasting and rearranging his whole life. The light of eternity, beating upon a human soul, often renders retreat the only honorable and courageous course.

F. W. Boreham, "On Climbing Down," *The Fiery Crags* (London: The Epworth Press, 1928), 77-86.

I.O.U.

I used to think—simple soul that I was!—that what every-body said must be true. Everybody said that it was very wicked to borrow. I therefore resolved, in the guilelessness of my soul, that, as long as I lived, I would never be guilty of such an offence. I need scarcely say that I have not kept that too heroic resolution. I have become an incorrigible borrower. I scarcely meet a man in the street but the sight of his face sets me calculating how much I owe him. I bor-row whenever and wherever I get the chance. I begin as soon as I rise in the morning, and I keep it up until the last thing at night. I began it before I got into my cradle; I shall continue it after I get out of my grave. I never pay for anything I purchase; at least, I only pay a part, and get credit for the rest. When I really must pay, I pay, if it be at all possible, as Mr. Micawber paid—with an I.O.U. Every-body knows the story. Mr. Micawber was leaving London; but he owed Mr. Traddles forty-one pounds ten shillings and eleven pence half-penny.

'To leave this metropolis,' said Mr. Micawber, 'and my friend Mr. Thomas Traddles, without acquitting myself of the pecuniary part of this obligation would weigh upon my mind to an insupportable extent. I have, therefore, prepared for my friend, Mr. Thomas Traddles, and I now hold in my hand, a document, which accomplishes the desired object. I beg to hand to my friend, Mr. Thomas Traddles, my I.O.U. for forty-one, ten, eleven and a half, and I am happy to recover my moral dignity, and to know that I can once more walk erect before my fellow man.'

With this introduction, which greatly affected him, Mr. Micawber placed his I.O.U. in the hands of Traddles, and said he wished him well in every relation of life. 'I am persuaded,' says David Copperfield, 'not only that this was quite the same to Mr. Micawber as paying the money, but that Traddles himself hardly knew the difference until he had had time to think about it. Mr. Micawber walked so erect before his fellow man, on the strength of this virtuous action, that his chest looked half as broad again when he lighted us down the stairs.' I take my stand this day, not only as Mr. Micawber's defender, but as his disciple. I am a convinced believer in the virtue of the I.O.U.

Some people may consider this a shocking state of things; but I am not in the least ashamed of it. I know that everybody still says that it is very wicked to borrow. I used to believe it; but I now smile up my sleeve. For since I first heard the statement that it is very wrong to borrow, I have knocked about the world a bit, and, in the process, have made several discoveries. I have discovered that, when everybody says a thing, and when everybody says it as confidently as if it were one of the Ten Commandments,

everybody is generally talking nonsense! I have discovered
that everybody else borrows, pretty much as I do; and that
those who are loudest in their denunciation of the habit
are often the most addicted to it; I have discovered that,
whether I borrow from other people or not, they will insist
on borrowing from me; and, in sheer self-protection, I am
driven to a policy of retaliation. And—to come still nearer
to the point—I have discovered that I must borrow or die;
and, as dying has no immediate attractions for me, I prefer
to borrow. I have referred to it as a habit. A habit it certainly
is. It is wonderful how it grows on you. I sometimes even
catch myself, as I shall presently explain, borrowing things
that I do not want, things for which I have no earthly use!
And now I have told the humiliating story. If it be true, as
everybody says, that open confession is good for the soul,
then my soul ought to enter upon a new lease of life as
a result of my having thus made a clean breast of things!
I began borrowing early. When I was making my plans
for invading this planet, I came to the conclusion that my
equipment would be very incomplete unless I brought a
body with me. In an earlier chapter of this book—that on
"The Enchanted Coat"—I have depicted the inconvenience
of being without one. But a body was the one thing that I
did not happen to possess. A body is composed, I was given
to understand, of certain chemical substances. It consists of
so much iron, so much phosphate, so much salt, so much
soda, and so on. Now here was a dilemma in which to be
placed at the very start! I could not begin without a body; a
body required all these substances, and I did not chance to
have any of them about me. What was I to do? I could only
borrow! But from whom? It is begging the issue to say that

I borrowed from my parents. They no more possessed these chemicals in their own right than I did. If they had them, it was because they too had borrowed them; and to the extent to which I borrowed from them, I merely borrowed what they had already borrowed. Iron, phosphate, salt, and all these chemicals belong to the earth beneath my feet; and, strictly speaking, it was from her that I borrowed my body. 'The Lord God formed man of the dust of the ground.' From the earth, then, I borrowed my body. It was distinctly a loan, and not a gift. I had to faithfully promise that, as soon as I have finished with it, I will return it to the earth again. 'Ashes to ashes, dust to dust.' The chemicals that I borrowed from the earth must all go back to the earth. Nature makes her advances only on the best security. She holds the mortgage in a very firm clutch, and will exact, to the uttermost farthing, all that she has lent.

It is so all through life. Never a day comes to me under these clear Australian skies but I am touched to tears at the memory of the goodness—the self-sacrificing goodness— that my father and mother lavished upon me in the dear old English home. But now that I have left them far behind across the seas, I find myself surrounded by happy children of my own. And I see now that, in those old untroubled days across the years, I was borrowing, merely borrowing. And all these smaller hands stretched out towards me are the hands that Nature has sent to demand the repayment of the loan. If I refuse to show them love and tenderness and sympathy, I shall feel like a man whose check has been dis-honored at the bank. The time has come for the repayment of the loan; I repudiate the obligation; and the faces of my father and my mother rise up in judgement against me.

Now, in glancing over what I have written, I see that I have made a pair of statements for which I shall certainly be taken to task. Let me therefore fortify them in anticipation of the inevitable assault. I declared that, so persistent does the borrowing habit become, it frequently leads me to borrow what I really do not want. That is an absolute fact. Instead of contenting myself with the worries of today, do I not very often borrow the burdens of tomorrow? I found myself the other evening staggering along under a load that was heavy enough to crush half a dozen strong men. Out of sheer exhaustion I put it down and had a good look at it. I found that it was all borrowed! Part of it belonged to the following day; part of it belonged to the following week; part of it belonged to the following year; and here was I borrowing it that it might crush me now! It is a very stupid, but a very ancient, blunder.

> There's a saying, old and rusty,
> But as good as any new;
> 'Tis 'Never trouble trouble
> Till trouble troubles you.'
>
> Don't you borrow sorrow;
> You'll surely have your share;
> He who dreams of sorrow
> Will find that sorrow's there.
>
> If care you've got to carry,
> Wait till 'tis at the door,
> For he who runs to meet it
> Takes up the load before.

This borrowing business must be done on very sane lines, or it leads to disaster. I know a man who borrows every Saturday all Sunday's energy; and on Sunday he is bankrupt. He would not dream of going to a picnic on Sunday afternoon, or of attending a picture-show on Sunday night. But he so exhausts himself on his picnics and his picture-shows on Saturday, that it takes all day Sunday to get over it. Our forefathers—the cotter of Burns's great poem and the rest—used to store up Saturday's energies so that they might be at their best on the Sunday. On the whole, I prefer their way of arranging the matter. When good old Dr. Johnson called himself to account, before entering on his fiftieth year, and set himself to live henceforth more devoutly, he wrote down, as the first step towards that high end, '*I resolve henceforth to go to sleep early on Saturday night.*' There is more sound philosophy in the great man's brave resolution than appears on the surface.

But I made one other statement that may be challenged. I said that I never pay for anything I purchase, but only pay a part of the price and get credit for the rest. That is quite true, and, as a consequence, I am in debt to all the world. What of the soldier who hazards his life in my defense? Do I dispose of my obligation to him when I pay my taxes? What of the miner who dares the perils of the mine? Do I square accounts with him when I pay my coal bill? And what of the toilers who obtain for me my food? James Nasmyth, the inventor of the steam-hammer, tells us in his autobiography of the picturesque scenes that he witnessed as a boy in the old fish market in Edinburgh. After a stormy night, he says, during which the husbands and sons had toiled at the risk of their lives to catch the fish, intending buyers would ask the usual question of the fish-wives:

'Weel, Janet, and hoo's haddies the day?'
'Haddies, mem?' Janet would reply meaningly,
'ou, haddies is men's lives the day!'

The shining fish would be sold, however, for a few coppers; but did those few coppers settle the score? 'How little we pay our way in life!' exclaims Robert Louis Stevenson, in *An Inland Voyage*. 'Although we have our purses continually in our hand, the better part of service still goes unrewarded.' Said I not truly that I never pay for anything I purchase, but only pay a part and get credit for the rest? Let me make no mistake. Unless I give back to the world something that costs me blood and agony and tears, I shall, when I quit the planet at last, be in the position of the man who leaves the neighborhood without first discharging his just and honorable debts. I set out, be it noted, to justify *borrowing*; I have nothing to say in defense of *theft*.

I knew a man once who thought it very wicked to borrow.

'My dear fellow,' I said, 'you can't get through life without it!'

'Oh!' he answered, visibly shocked, 'but does not the Bible exhort us *to owe no man anything?*'

'No,' I replied, 'the Bible says nothing of the kind. The Bible says, "Owe no man anything *but—,*" and that exception is the greatest exception to a general principle that has ever been stated in human language. "Owe no man anything, *but to love one another.*"' And since then he has been struggling bravely to discharge that tremendous obligation.

F. W. Boreham, "I.O.U.," *The Other Side of the Hill* (London: Charles H. Kelly, 1917), 103-111.

THE BENEDICTION

It is not often that a minister sits among his people listening to the voice of another. That rare privilege fell to my lot last Sunday; and how thoroughly I enjoyed it my friends know very well. The hymns, the prayers, the sermon—each part of the service in its turn—seemed wonderfully refreshing and uplifting; and the Benediction seemed the climax of the whole. The feeling may have arisen from that sweet sadness which invariably enfolds the last moments of all earthly pleasures; or it may have been that there really is a grandeur in those stately cadences that had never before so powerfully impressed me. However that may be, I shall never forget that hushed and solemn moment in which, the congregation standing with bowed heads, the minister pronounced those sublime simplicities, those simple sublimities. Like the breath of heaven there fell upon us those ancient but wealthy words:

The grace of the Lord Jesus Christ, and the love of God, and the communion of the Holy Ghost, be with you all. Amen.

A moment's stillness followed; and then we quietly turned homewards; but, whichever way we went, the tender grace of that beauteous benediction seemed to follow and enfold us.

I

I suppose that the simple words derive their grandeur from the fact that they state, with the grace of the poet rather than with the technique of the theologian, the mystery of the Trinity. It is an awful theme, and suited only to just such a setting. There are things which, like the song of the lark and the perfume of the violet, do not lend themselves to definition. When I let my mind play about that stupendous thought which is embalmed in the phraseology of the Benediction, I fancy that my modest ventures in photography have given me a hint or two towards its comprehension. For my camera has taught me that there are three ways of looking at everything. There are—

1. The Way of my Right Eye.
2. The Way of my Left Eye.
3. The Way of my Camera.

That the way of the right eye differs from the way of the left eye can be demonstrated by the simple process of closing each of the eyes in turn, and examining the object first with the one eye only and then with the other eye only. Each sees the thing from its own angle. The camera cannot adjust itself to both eyes, so it effects a compromise. Its single lens sees things as they would appear to me if I had but one eye, and that one eye in the middle of my forehead. But, obviously, no one of these three ways is, in itself, the correct way of looking at a thing. As I reflect thus, along comes my more fortunate friend with a stereoscopic camera. He takes, not one view which is a compromise between my right eye's view and my left eye's view, but two views— the view of the object as my right eye sees it and the view of the object as my left eye sees it. Then he places the two views behind glasses, which, applied to my two eyes, blend the two into one, just as my eyes are accustomed automatically to do. The result is that the picture is real and vivid and lifelike. I tried, once upon a day, to think of God the Father, and to think of God the Son, and to think of God the Holy Spirit. But I became hopelessly confused. And then I heard the voice of Jesus declare that 'He that hath seen Me hath seen the Father,' and I understood that in the person of Jesus I have the stereoscopic view of God.

II

And then, as I walked home from church, with the music of the Benediction ringing in my ears, it seemed like a declaration that all the treasure of heaven is for each mortal on earth. 'The grace of the Lord Jesus Christ, and the love of God, and the communion of the Holy Ghost, *be with you all.*' The best things are indivisible. If you divide *material* treasure between a thousand people, each has a thousandth part; but if you divide the *heavenly* treasure between a thousand people, each has the whole.

I am very fond of that fine passage in the *Compleat Angler* in which the gentle author tells of the delight that he found in thousands of things that did not strictly belong to him. The actual owner of the estate on which he fished was worried to death by vexatious disputes and threatened litigation; but, as for Izaak, he was in the seventh heaven. He strolled down through the leafy woods and shady groves; he crossed the fragrant meadows in which he saw a tousle-haired schoolboy gathering lilies and a rosy-cheeked lassie with an armful of cowslips; he cast his line into the sparkling stream and saw the great silvery trout flash through the laughing waters; and he was in bliss without alloy. 'As I sat thus,' he says, 'joying in my own happy condition, and pitying this poor rich man that owned this and many other pleasant groves and meadows about me, I did thankfully remember that my Savior said that the meek possess the earth. Anglers and meek, quiet-spirited men are free from those high and restless thoughts which corrode the sweets of life, and they therefore enjoy what others possess and enjoy not.' Is it not true that, in the best things, the whole is for each? The truest treasure is indivisible. What is it that Miss Ella Wheeler Wilcox sings in her poem, "All for Me"?

> The world grows green on a thousand hills—
> By a thousand willows the bees are humming,
> And a million birds by a million rills
> Sing of the golden season coming.
> But, gazing out on the sun-kissed lea,
> And hearing a thrush and a bluebird singing,
> I feel that the summer is all for me,
> And all for me the joys it is bringing.

All for me the bumble-bee
Drones his song in the perfect weather
And, just on purpose to sing to me,
Thrush and bluebird come here together.

Just for me, in red and white,
Bloom and blossom the fields of clover;
And all for me and my delight
The wild wind follows and plays the lover.

Yes, all for me, all for me, *all for me!* That was what I caught myself saying to myself as I walked home from church in the sunshine of that spring Sunday morning. The grace of our Lord Jesus Christ—all for me, all for me! And the love of God—all for me, all for me! And the communion of the Holy Ghost—all for me, all for me; 'The grace of our Lord Jesus Christ, and the love of God, and the communion of the Holy Ghost, be with you all.' Yes, with us all—it was all for me, *all for me!*

III

This was good, but better was to come. For, just as I came in sight of the golden wattle beside my own gate, another thought arrested me. Looking at the Benediction once again, I saw that it is not so much the Father and the Son and the Holy Ghost who are to be with me; but the grace of the Savior and the love of the Father and the communion of the Holy Ghost. The service that I have just attended must leave its fragrance, that is to say, upon my own spirit. It is as though the preacher had said, 'You have been rejoicing in the inexhaustible grace of Jesus: now be yourself gracious!

You have been in the presence of God, and God is love: now be yourself tender-hearted and affectionate! You have enjoyed the radiant fellowship of the Holy Spirit: now be yourself companionable and inspiring!' I remember to have read of a Valley of Roses. It is so extensive, and the lovely odors hang so heavily about the beauteous vale, that the traveler who passes through it carries the perfume on his person for days afterwards, and people look knowingly at each other as he enters the room. They know without being told that he has been in the Valley of Roses. As I projected my memory back to that tense closing moment of the service I had left, it seemed as though the Benediction was an exhortation. It called upon me to share with others the boon that had been mine, by carrying with me the fragrance in which I had been reveling. It seemed, as I contemplated my restless spirit and my dusty heart, a mere counsel of perfection; and yet, and yet—

> A Persian fable says: One day
> A wanderer found a piece of clay
> So redolent of sweet perfume
> Its odor scented all the room.
> 'What art thou!' was the quick demand,
> 'Art thou some gem from Samarcand?
> Or spikenard rare in rich disguise?
> Or other costly merchandise ?'
> 'Nay, I am but a piece of clay!'
> 'Then whence this wondrous sweetness, pray?'
> 'Friend, if the secret I disclose,
> I have been dwelling with a rose!'

I fancy that is what the preacher meant. If, within the house of the Lord, I had been really enjoying the society of that holy Savior who is Himself the fountain of all grace, surely I must thereafter be *myself* more gracious! If, during those hallowed moments, I had gazed upon the Love that will not let me go, surely I must thereafter be *myself* more loving! If, there in the sanctuary, I had reveled in the fellowship of the Comforter, surely there can be no soul beneath the stars to whom I can henceforth deny my own sympathy and friendship. Yes, that was what the preacher meant—'*The grace of the Lord Jesus Christ, and the love of God, and the communion of the Holy Ghost, be with you all. Amen.*' And as I put my hand to the latch of my own gate, I involuntarily murmured '*Amen*' a second time.

F. W. Boreham, "The Benediction," *The Other Side of the Hill* (London: Charles H. Kelly, 1917), 265-272.

ABOUT THE COVER

"Packet" makes me think of a package of seeds. You sow a seed, but what springs up looks much different. The difference between the body of the seed and the body of the plant is somewhat of a surprise.

I still remember my pleasant surprise at reading Boreham for the first time. My heart was "strangely warmed" as I read through "Thomas Chalmers' Text" in *Life Verses Volume One*.

Here was a writer that combined so many elements that move me deeply: story, history, illustration, poetry, beauty, quotations and more. I had forgotten how much I liked wonder-filled literature, and reading the lovely story of Thomas Chalmers woke me from slumber. It felt like a new day. I devoured the rest of the book and series.

What a surprise to find such treasure in the writings of a man, who but for the frequent mentions of his name by Ravi Zacharias, might be mostly forgotten.

I'm so glad for the image of the flower that has yet to unfold its petals. The glory of its blossom is about to be revealed. What it will be is not yet fully known. It beautifully conveys the surprise and wonder that I hope every reader finds in these essays and sermons.

May Boreham's thoughts, like seeds, take root and grow in our hearts so that the beauty of the flower brings glory to its Maker.

Michael Dalton

PUBLISHER'S NOTE

We are grateful to Dr. Frank Rees at Whitley College for the permission to publish this book and for the practical support given by the College. Permission to reproduce significant portions of this book can be obtained from Whitley College, 271 Royal Parade, Parkville, Australia, 3052.

A portion of the sale of each book will go toward the training of pastors and missionaries at Whitley College, a ministry that F. W. Boreham supported during his lifetime.

Essays in this volume are drawn from books previously published by Epworth Press.

Sincere thanks to Laura Zugzda for the cover design, Stephanie Martindale for layout and Jeff Cranston and Brian Gish for proofing.

Further information about the life and work of F. W. Boreham is available at the F. W. Boreham Facebook page: http://www.facebook.com/pages/F-W-Boreham/121475236386 and THE OFFICIAL F W BOREHAM BLOG SITE: http://fwboreham.blogspot.com.

Your comments and questions are welcome and they can be addressed to:

Michael Dalton
John Broadbanks Publishing
2163 Fern Street
Eureka, CA 95503, USA
dalton.michael@sbcglobal.net

Geoff Pound
c/o HCT,
PO Box 4114
FUJAIRAH,
United Arab Emirates
geoffpound@gmail.com

Jeff Cranston
LowCountry Community Church
801 Buckwalter Parkway, Bluffton, SC 29910
jcranston@lowcountrycc.org
www.lowcountrycc.org

TOPICAL INDEX

NAME INDEX